# Contents

# List of Figures and Tables

# List of Contributors

| | |
|---|---|
| **Authors:** | Sarah Armitage, NHS Direct |
| | Rachel Barker, Department for Education and Skills |
| | Ivan Bishop, Department of Trade and Industry |
| | Iain Bryson, Department of Finance and Personnel, Northern Ireland |
| | Tony Clayton |
| | Lindsay Clothier, Department for Environment, Food and Rural Affairs |
| | Christina Forrest |
| | Joe Gardiner, Department of Trade and Industry |
| | Mark Leaver |
| | Ewen McKinnon, Cabinet Office |
| | Mark Pollard |
| | Adrian Shepherd |
| | Debbie Wilson, Home Office |
| | |
| **Production Manager:** | Chris Randall |
| | |
| **Production Assistant:** | Steve Whyman |
| | |
| **Reviewers:** | Jonathan Knight |
| | Helen Meaker |
| | Nina Mill |
| | Cecil Prescott |

# Acknowledgements

The editors wish to thank all the authors of individual chapters, and colleagues in the Office for National Statistics who have helped in the preparation of this report.

We are also grateful to our colleagues from other government departments and agencies for their generous support and helpful comments:

Cabinet Office

Department for Education and Skills

Department for Environment, Food and Rural Affairs

Department of Trade and Industry

Home Office

NHS Direct

Northern Ireland Statistics and Research Agency

# Symbols and Conventions

*Rounding of figures.* In tables where figures have been rounded to the nearest final digit, there may be an apparent discrepancy between the sum of the constituent items and the total as shown.

*Billion.* This term is used to represent a thousand million.

*Provisional and estimated data.* Some data for the latest year (and occasionally for earlier years) are provisional or estimated. To keep footnotes to a minimum, these have not been indicated in the figures and tables. Source departments will be able to advise if revised data are available.

*Financial year.* (April to March) is shown as, for example, 2004/05.

*Academic year.* (September to July) is shown as, for example 2004/05.

*Combined years.* (Data for more than one year) are shown as, for example, 2003–05.

*Data covering more than one year.* For example 2001, 2002 and 2003 are shown as 2001 to 2003

*Units on tables.* Where one unit predominates it is shown at the top of the table. All other units are shown against the relevant row or column. Figures are shown in italics when they represent percentages.

*Symbols in tables.* The following symbols have been used:

- -  negligible

- 0  nil

Introduction

The rapid take up of information and communication technology (ICT) by individuals since the 1990s has changed the way people can communicate with each other, the way they can gain access to information, goods and services, and the way they spend their leisure time. ICT includes computers, digital television, digital video disc (DVD) players/recorders, digital radio, mobile phones and the Internet. The adoption of ICT in schools and colleges is also having an effect on education across the curriculum. Similarly in business and in government adoption of ICT has led to changing working practices, new products and the need for different skills. These changes are widespread across society and the economy.

It is called the digital age because most ICT relies on digital signals, which reduce information to a binary series of zeroes and ones. Before digital technology was introduced, most communication was conducted by analogue technology, which produces a signal along a continuum.

ICT has a number of features that distinguish it from older communication technology such as fixed-line telephones, traditional television and radio, and video cassette recorders. It is more versatile than previous communication technology. ICT can be used in more than one place: computers can be portable; phones can be mobile. Traditional communication technology tended to be limited to one location and one use. Digital communication is easier to send than analogue and allows an increased flow of information. Different types of information, including text, sound, graphics and video, can all be reduced to a series of zeroes and ones and so can be sent digitally. This has led to technology being developed that can send and receive different types of content, a process known as convergence. For example, as well as making calls, mobile phones can send text messages and provide a range of services including connecting to the Internet and taking and sending pictures.

ICT allows more people to create new information, provides convenient access to information, and enables consumers to interact with information produced by others, especially on the Internet. Using the Internet, any person or organisation with sufficient technical ability and a small amount of money can produce a web-page that can be accessed by any Internet user. Unless access to a web-page is deliberately restricted, an Internet user can visit any web-page at any time. Through the Internet, people can read and download content. They can also input information, such as shopping orders or written messages. Using email, one person can communicate and send messages to another person or to many people.

Traditional television and radio programmes are accessed at the time that they are broadcast, with video and cassette recording giving the consumer some control over when they watch or listen to programmes. Digital television and radio services allow a greater number of channels to be broadcast, providing scope for a larger number of companies to create material that goes on air. With digital technology, a consumer can also interact with the information being provided. With a digital television service, a viewer can vote in or answer polls. With computer games, the player can control a character that is involved with the game.

## Government policy

In the 1998 Queen's Speech the Government expressed its belief in the importance of ICT to future economic prosperity. Government policy is to encourage the growth of Internet access and use. In 2000 it set a target that Internet access should be available for all who wanted it in the UK by 2005. By 2006 public Internet access was available through almost all public libraries, online centres, and some post offices. The Government also had a target that every community in the country should have broadband capability. By the beginning of 2006 more than 97 per cent of households and businesses were able to receive broadband.

The Government has encouraged widespread learning of e-skills so individuals could benefit more from using computers and the Internet. It has classified e-skills as the third area of adult basic skills, alongside literacy and numeracy.[1] One aspect of this objective was to ensure that schoolchildren had access to the Internet at school, and that all primary and secondary schools had broadband access.

Another target was to make all government services electronically available. Government web-sites include NHS Direct Online where people can find health information, Direct Government where people can access government services such as booking a driving test or renewing a passport, and ChildcareLink where people can get information about local child care facilities.

The Government provides the legal framework for the use of ICT to overcome problems such as the security of online payments and the enforcement of copyright law, particularly in respect of music being downloaded from the Internet. Legislation also ensures the protection of the privacy of personal data stored online, and protection of Internet users from harmful or unpleasant communication such as computer viruses and unwanted emails advertising products for sale (known as spam).

## Contents and structure

*Focus on the Digital Age* has been produced in response to an increasing demand for statistics and analyses on the use of ICT by individuals, schools, business and government in the UK.

This report aims to capture the fundamentals of the digital age. The different chapters show the extent to which people and businesses have taken up the new technology, and what kind of people and businesses they are. It analyses how ICT is changing the ways people can communicate with each other, shop, and find out information. It looks at how ICT is changing business practices and altering relations between government and the people. It compares the use of ICT in the UK with that in other countries and describes the problems that the digital age has brought about.

*Focus on the Digital Age* has eight chapters. Chapter 1 outlines the different ICT, the range of functions and services available, and their rapid take-up by individuals and households over the last decade. Chapter 2 focuses on individual and household use of the Internet. This looks at what kind of people are likely to be Internet users, how and where they go online and what activities they do online.

The extent to which schools and colleges have incorporated ICT into their everyday work and the impact this has had on pupils, students and teachers is assessed in Chapter 3. It also discusses demand for ICT skills in the workplace.

Chapter 4 looks at ICT and business. It shows the proportion of businesses that use different types of ICT and how this has changed over time. It also describes how businesses in different sectors of the economy and of different sizes vary in their use of ICT.

The wider impact of ICT on the UK economy is examined in Chapter 5. This includes how much of the investment and growth in the UK over the last decade has been accounted for by ICT, how it has affected productivity, and e-commerce.

Chapter 6 compares the adoption and use of ICT in the UK with that of other countries. It evaluates how the adoption of ICT affects the behaviour of multinational companies and 'outsourcing', the location of business services abroad.

Online government services for both individuals and businesses are covered in Chapter 7, along with who uses them and who does not. It includes case studies of the NHS Direct Online and Businesslink.gov.uk.

Chapter 8 looks at the online security issues faced by Internet users, both individuals and businesses, including the prevalence of computer viruses, credit card fraud, spam, copyright theft, theft of equipment and denial of service.

ICT covers a wide field and *Focus on the Digital Age* does not attempt to cover everything. The report focuses on how people are taking up the new technology, and on how people are changing their behaviour as a result of the technology becoming available. Although much of the technology has been developed quite recently, where possible time series are used to show how the use of ICT has changed.

*Focus on the Digital Age* draws together statistics from a range of government departments and other organisations. It is aimed at a general audience and presents data as figures and tables with explanatory text that is easy to understand. Expertise in computers, the Internet and other technology is not required to understand the report. Nor is expertise in statistics. The report provides a resource for all those with an interest in ICT, including policy-makers, researchers, journalists, students and members of the public.

We welcome feedback on this report. Please email: eSociety@ons.gov.uk or write to:

Economic Surveys
Surveys and Administrative Sources
Office for National Statistics
Room 2364
Government Buildings
Cardiff Road
Newport
South Wales, NP10 8XG

## Notes and references

1. Department for Education and Skills White Paper, 2003. *21st Century Skills, Realising Our Potential*, p 25.

# Use of ICT among Households and Individuals

**Adrian Shepherd**
Office for National Statistics

Chapter 1

# Introduction

Personal computers became available in the 1970s and compact disc (CD) players and discs in the 1980s. Other information and communication technology (ICT), including the Internet, digital mobile phones, digital video disc (DVD) players, digital television service and digital radio service, have only been available since the 1990s. Use of ICT has grown rapidly in the last decade and ICT has become an integral part of many people's lives. Although digital technology is relatively new, it is already approaching the near universal levels of use of older technologies, such as analogue television or the telephone.

In 2005/06, 88 per cent of UK households owned a CD player and 79 per cent a mobile phone (Figure 1.1). Growth in ownership of a DVD player increased sharply over recent years, with the proportion of households owning one rising by more than one-and-a-half-times between 2002/03 and 2005/06, from 31 per cent to 79 per cent. Household Internet access grew from 10 per cent in 1998/99 to 55 per cent in 2005/06. The fastest annual growth was in the 12 months to March 2001, when the proportion of households with Internet access grew by 13 percentage points. Growth subsequently slowed and the proportion rose by 2 per cent in the 12 months to March 2006. Ownership of a digital television service grew steadily, from 19 per cent of households in 1996/97 to 65 per cent of households in 2005/06.

## Figure **1.1**

### Households with selected ICT[1]

**United Kingdom**

Percentages

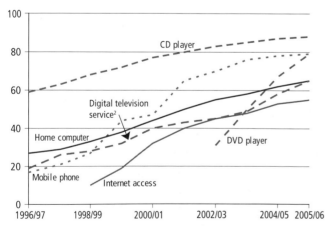

1   Based on weighted data. Data for 1998/99 onwards include children's expenditure.
2   Includes digital, satellite and cable receivers.

*Source: Family Expenditure Survey and Expenditure and Food Survey, Office for National Statistics*

Household ownership of personal computers and Internet access are closely associated and both are linked to household income. Household ownership of mobile phones and a digital television service in the UK are also linked to income, although to a lesser extent than personal computers and Internet access (Figure 1.2). In 2005/06 households in the highest income decile group[1] were around five-and-a-half-times as likely as those in the lowest income decile group to have an Internet connection, 93 per cent of households compared with 17 per cent. Households in the highest income group were nearly twice as likely to have a digital television service, and around one-and-a-half-times as likely as households in the lowest income decile group to have a mobile phone.

## Figure **1.2**

### Household ownership of selected ICT: by income group, 2005/06

**United Kingdom**

Percentage

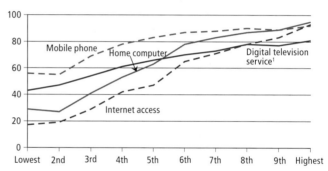

1   Includes digital, satellite and cable receivers.

*Source: Expenditure and Food Survey, Office for National Statistics*

There is considerable overlap in the ownership of ICT (Figure 1.3). In January to April 2006,[2] 45 per cent of households in Great Britain received a digital television service, owned a mobile phone and had access to the Internet. A higher proportion (18 per cent) of households had access to both a digital television service and a mobile phone, but not to the Internet, than those with access to the Internet and a mobile phone, but not to a digital television service (11 per cent). Among households with Internet access, 97 per cent also had access to mobile phones. The majority of households without access to a mobile phone also lacked access to the Internet (87 per cent), while 8 per cent of households did not have access to a digital television service, a mobile phone, or the Internet.

Recently a process known as convergence has begun to blur the distinctions between different forms of digital ICT so that one type of ICT can perform a variety of functions. Some mobile phones, for example, can be used to access the Internet, send and receive emails, and send and receive digital photographs, as well as to make telephone calls and send and receive texts. A digital television service or games console can also be used to access the Internet.

**Figure 1.3**

## Household access to various ICT,[1] 2006[2]

**Great Britain**

Percentages

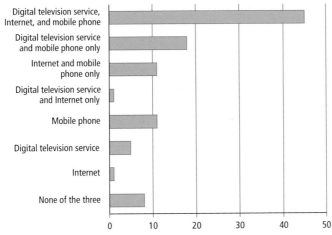

1  Digital television service, Internet and mobile phone.
2  Data collected in January, February and April.

*Source: Omnibus Survey, Office for National Statistics*

## Personal computers and the Internet

Until Internet use became widespread in the late 1990s, personal computers were used mainly for word-processing, desktop publishing, playing games and managing databases. In 1998/99, one-third (33 per cent) of households in the UK possessed a personal computer. This had nearly doubled to 65 per cent of households by 2005/06.

There are essentially three types of personal computer, based on size: desktop computers, portable or laptop computers, and palmtop or handheld computers, also called personal digital assistants (PDAs). In January to April 2006, 56 per cent of households in Great Britain had a desktop computer, 30 per cent had a portable or laptop computer, and 7 per cent had a handheld computer.

In January to April 2006, 76 per cent of adults in Great Britain had ever used a computer and 67 per cent had used one within the last three months. Computer use varies by age. The majority of people aged between 16 and 30 (87 per cent) had used a computer in the last three months compared with 45 per cent of those aged 50 and over.

The Internet is one way that people can communicate with one another through ICT and primarily consists of email and the world wide web (see also Chapter 2: Household and Individual Use of the Internet). The world wide web, also known as www or the web, was developed in the late 1980s. It has its origins in computer networks developed by the US Defence Department in the 1960s. The network gradually extended in use to academia, government, business and individuals.

The world wide web is information available on the Internet that can be accessed by software called a web-browser. It consists of web-pages containing text, graphics, photos, film, sound and other media. Web-pages and web-browsers were developed in their current form during 1993 and 1994.

Web-pages are produced by content-providers; these can be government departments, organisations, businesses, societies and individuals. Web-pages can be linked allowing users to move directly from one to another. Each page has an address allowing direct access (unless access is restricted, perhaps through the use of a password). Users have different levels of familiarity with computers. By January to April 2006, 9 per cent of adults in Great Britain had created a web-page. As well as accessing web-pages and sending emails, the Internet also supports other forms of communication and entertainment (see Chapter 2: Online activities).

Growth in individual Internet use has come from those who can go online in their own home. The home is the most common place for people to access the Internet (see Chapter 2: Accessing the Internet). Although the Internet can be accessed using a mobile phone, a digital television service, games console, and other technology, using a computer is the most common way to go online.

According to the Media Literacy Audit published by the Office of Communications (Ofcom)[3] in 2006, the main reasons why people in the UK acquired Internet access at home was for the content or information available through the Internet (46 per cent), communication (28 per cent), keeping up with technology (22 per cent) and acquiring it for their children (20 per cent).

In January to April 2006, 52 per cent of adults in Great Britain had used the Internet in the three months before interview and lived in households with Internet access (Figure 1.4). This was up from 37 per cent in 2001/02. The proportion of adults who used the Internet but who lived in households without Internet access went down slightly over the same period, from 11 to 7 per cent. Adults who were not Internet users and who lived in households with Internet access remained constant at around 9 per cent. Between January and April 2006, 31 per cent of adults were not Internet users and lived in a household without Internet access, down from 43 per cent in 2001/02.

3

# Figure **1.4**

## Current Internet use[1] and home Internet access[2]

**Great Britain**

Percentages

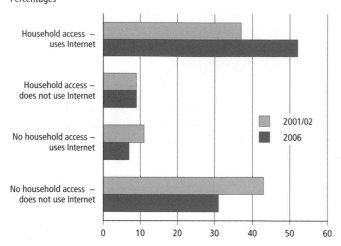

1   Current Internet users are defined as those who have gone online in the last three months.
2   Data for 2001/02 were collected in April, July, October and February. Data for 2006 were collected in January, February and April.

*Source: Omnibus Survey, Office for National Statistics*

## Mobile phones

Mobile phones are one of the most widely used of the contemporary ICT. The first digital mobile phone was introduced in the UK in 1991. Digital mobile phones have several advantages over earlier analogue ones. The handsets are more compact, they have clearer voice quality, better call security, and more extensive and reliable network coverage.

There has been rapid growth in the proportion of UK households owning a mobile phone, although the rate of growth has recently slowed (see Figure 1.1). In 1996/97, 17 per cent of households owned a mobile phone. This increased to 65 per cent of households in 2001/02 and continued to increase, although more slowly, to 79 per cent in 2005/06.

The 2006 Media Literacy Audit found a strong link between a mobile phone user's age and the reasons for owning a mobile phone. Adults aged 55 and over were likely to have a mobile phone for use in emergency, while people aged under 35 were likely to acquire a mobile phone for keeping in touch with friends and family and the younger adults, aged under 25, acquired their mobile phone for the purpose of texting.

Most households with mobile phones also have fixed line telephones. In January to April 2006, 77 per cent of households in Great Britain had both mobile and fixed line telephones (Figure 1.5). A greater proportion of households (13 per cent) had only a fixed line telephone, while 9 per cent of households had a mobile phone only and 2 per cent had no telephone in the household.

# Figure **1.5**

## Household ownership of fixed and mobile telephones, 2006[1]

**Great Britain**

Percentages

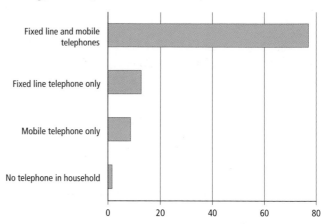

1   Data collected in January, February and April.

*Source: Omnibus Survey, Office for National Statistics*

## Functions available on mobile phones

The range of functions available on mobile phones continues to develop. In January to April 2006, 30 per cent of households in Great Britain possessed a mobile phone that could access the Internet. This was up from 20 per cent in April 2003. In January to April 2006, 11 per cent of adults had used a mobile phone to browse the Internet in the three months before interview.

Another function available on mobile phones is the Short Messaging Service (SMS), also known as texting, which was introduced in 1994. This allows a mobile phone user to send and receive a short written message from other mobile phones. In July 2005,[4] 66 per cent of adults in Great Britain had sent a text, and 68 per cent had received one. Mobile phone users can also receive texts as part of an information service, for example, news headlines, traffic updates, or sports information. In July 2005, 7 per cent of adults subscribed to such services. As well as voice and text, mobile phones that include Multimedia Messaging Service (MMS) can also send pictures. In July 2005, 28 per cent of adults had sent a digital photograph using their mobile phone and 27 per cent had received one. Other functions that are available on some mobile phones, or are being developed, include games, radio, music and television.

The most common reasons why adult mobile phone users in the UK used a mobile phone in 2005, according to the 2006 Media Literacy Audit, were making personal or business calls (85 per cent of mobile phone users) and sending personal or business text messages (70 per cent). However, these uses differed according to age; 94 per cent of young people aged between 16 and 24 sent personal or business text messages compared with 17 per cent of those aged 65 and over (Figure 1.6). Young people in the 16 to 24 age group were also more likely than those aged 65 and over to use their mobile phone to make business or personal calls, 93 per cent compared with 58 per cent, and to take photos using their mobile phones, 58 per cent compared with 2 per cent.

## Figure **1.6**

### Different uses of mobile phone: by selected age groups, 2005

**United Kingdom**

Percentages

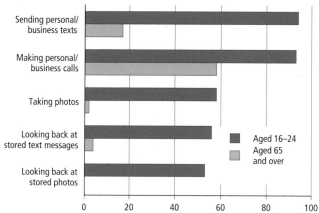

Source: 2006 Media Literacy Audit, Ofcom

## Digital television

Ownership of a digital television service has increased. Nearly two-thirds (65 per cent) of households in the UK received a digital television service in 2005/06 compared with 19 per cent in 1996/97, when data on this were first collected. There was a large increase in households with a digital television service between 1999/2000 and 2000/01, from 32 per cent to 40 per cent, and again between 2003/04 and 2004/05 from 49 to 58 per cent.

Digital television can be received in a number of different ways: by satellite, cable, or through a digital terrestrial service. It can also be accessed using an asymmetric digital subscriber line (ADS), which uses telephone lines to access television. The Government plans to implement a 'digital switchover' after which analogue terrestrial broadcasting will cease and television signals will only be received digitally. The digital switchover will occur between 2008 and 2012, the exact date varying by region.

According to Ofcom,[5] switching over to a digital television service would have several benefits. Consumers would have access to a wider range of channels, including a range of free-to-view channels, and radio services. A digital television service would provide better quality of sound and picture than traditional analogue television, and would offer consumers access to a number of interactive services.

The first digital television service in the UK was launched in 1997 and the first digital satellite service in 1998. Satellite television had previously existed in analogue form, and this continued alongside digital satellite television until 2001. Cable television services also exist in analogue form, but digital cable services are more common. In 2002 digital terrestrial services were launched in their current form, as Freeview. Freeview is a service that provides more than 40 free digital television channels, as well as radio and interactive services, through a normal television aerial.

The 2006 Media Literacy Audit found that the most common reasons why people acquired a digital television service in the UK were to receive more channels (69 per cent) or to receive particular channels (21 per cent) (Figure 1.7). These were followed by quality of picture (15 per cent). A digital television service also allows viewers to interact with the television. Nearly one-third of those with a digital television service had interacted using the red button as a result of seeing something on screen. Interaction is most common among people aged 25 to 34, with over one-half (52 per cent) having done so. The main reasons for digital interaction were to enter a competition or to find out about something featured on television (both 32 per cent) and to vote for or nominate someone (31 per cent).

Interactive services available on digital television include shopping, banking, getting details of government services and

## Figure **1.7**

### Reasons for acquiring a digital television service, 2005

**United Kingdom**

Percentages

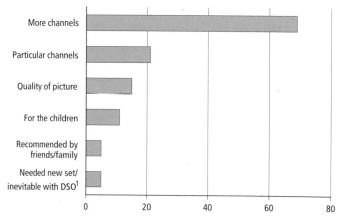

1 Digital switchover.

Source: 2006 Media Literacy Audit, Ofcom

taxes, texting, sending emails, voting on questions or issues and taking part in game shows. The availability of interactive services on digital television varies by the company that provides the service. In July 2005,[6] 33 per cent of adults in Great Britain with a television in their home could take part in game shows, and 28 per cent could buy products through shopping channels. This compared with 7 per cent who actually had taken part in game shows and 5 per cent who had bought products through shopping channels.

## Digital radio, DVDs and CDs

Digital Audio Broadcasting (DAB), also known as digital radio, offers better clarity and suffers less from interference than analogue radio. Digital radio broadcasts require less spectrum than traditional radio allowing more radio channels to occupy the same amount of space. Digital radio can also be received by digital television, over the Internet, and by mobile phone. According to the Radio Joint Audience Research (RAJAR), 15 per cent of people aged 15 and over in the UK lived in households with DAB between April and June 2006; 39 per cent had listened to the radio through a digital television and 23 per cent had listened through the Internet. Around 14 per cent of all radio listening during this period was through a digital channel.

By far the main reasons for acquiring digital radio for people who owned one in the UK in 2005 were better sound quality (42 per cent) and receiving more stations (31 per cent), according to the 2006 Media Literacy Audit.

Like the analogue video cassette recorder (VCR), the digital video disc (DVD) player allows people to play audio and visual material at their leisure. Some DVD players also record from the television. Advantages of the DVD over the VCR include better quality of sound and picture, longer recording time on each disc, lower levels of deterioration if stored over time and less space needed for storage. The proportion of households in the UK with a VCR increased from 86 per cent in 1998/99 to 90 per cent in 2003/04 and then began to fall, back to 86 per cent in 2005/06. DVD players were introduced in 1998 and by 2005/06, 79 per cent of households owned one.

The compact disc (CD) is an older digital technology than the DVD or digital radio, reaching a mass market during the 1980s. Primarily used for playing music, CDs can also be used on computers to record and play back information in a variety of different forms, such as audio or textual. Before the CD the main ways of playing music were the phonograph record and the tape cassette The advantage of the CD is superior sound quality. In 1996/97, 59 per cent of households in the UK owned a CD player. This had risen to 88 per cent in 2005/06.

In 1998 the first MP3 players were produced. The most popular of these is the hard drive-based player. These players read digital audio files from a hard drive. Thousands of songs, perhaps an entire music collection, can be stored on one MP3 player. According to RAJAR over one-quarter (26 per cent) of people aged 15 and over in the UK owned an MP3 player in April to June 2006. Of these 15 per cent had used their MP3 players to listen to downloaded radio programme podcasts.[7]

## Notes and references

1   One method of analysing income distribution is to rank units (households, individuals, etc) by a given income measure and then divide the ranked units into groups of equal size. Decile groups are groups that contain 10 per cent of units.

2   Data were collected in January, February and April 2006.

3   Ofcom (Office of Communications) is the independent regulator and competition authority for the UK communications industry. For more information about the Media Literacy Audit see www.ofcom.org.uk

4   July 2005 was the last time that the Omnibus Survey asked questions regarding use of functions available on mobile phones.

5   *Driving digital switchover: a report to the Secretary of State.* Ofcom, 2004. www.ofcom.org.uk

6   July 2005 was the last time that the Omnibus Survey asked what respondents had actually done regarding interaction on digital television.

7   Podcasting is a method of publishing files to the Internet. Users can subscribe and receive new files automatically, usually at no cost.

# Household and Individual Use of the Internet

**Adrian Shepherd**
Office for National Statistics
**Iain Bryson**
Department of Finance and Personnel,
Northern Ireland

Chapter 2

## Introduction

Use of the Internet is a key part of the digital age. There are different ways to measure people's use of the Internet. One is to ask them whether they have ever used the Internet. Another is to ask if they have gone online recently, usually within the last three months. This attempts to distinguish occasional use from current use.

### Current Internet users

In this chapter current Internet users are defined as adults aged 16 and over who reported that they had gone online during the three months before interview.

In January to April 2006[1] the proportion of adults in Great Britain who had ever used the Internet was 64 per cent, while 60 per cent were current Internet users (Figure 2.1). These proportions had risen from 55 per cent and 48 per cent respectively in 2001/02. The rise in the proportion of people who use the Internet appears to have levelled off between 2004/05 and January to April 2006.

### Figure 2.1

**Internet use: when adults[1] last went online[2]**

**Great Britain**
Percentages

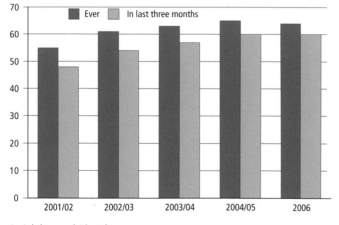

1  Adults aged 16 and over.
2  Data for 2001/02, 2002/03, 2003/04 and 2004/05 were collected in April (May in 2005), July, October and February. Data for 2006 were collected in January, February and April.

*Source: Omnibus Survey, Office for National Statistics*

## Accessing the Internet

Different types of information and communication technology (ICT) can be used to access the Internet. In 2004/05,[2] 94 per cent of adults who were current users of the Internet went online using a desktop computer, 29 per cent used a portable computer, 14 per cent used a mobile phone, 3 per cent a palmtop or handheld computer, and 2 per cent a digital television. Most current users (84 per cent) went online only

using a computer, while 15 per cent used more than one device to access the Internet. There has been a rise in the proportion of households where individuals can use mobile phones or a digital television service to access the Internet. In 2002/03, 3 per cent of households owned mobile phones that could be used to go online and 3 per cent had a digital television service that could access the Internet. By January to April 2006 these proportions had increased to 13 per cent and 5 per cent respectively (see also Chapter 1: Mobile phones, and Digital television).

Home is the most common location for adult Internet users of all ages to access the Internet. In January to April 2006, 85 per cent of current Internet users aged 16 and over went online at home. Home Internet connection offers the advantages of being convenient and private. In addition, there are no formal restrictions on web-pages that can be visited or on online actions, as there are at public libraries or some workplaces. However, one-third of people who used the Internet at home had taken measures to stop household members accessing or receiving offensive, pornographic or threatening material (see also Chapter 8: Offensive material through the Internet).

The proportion of adult Internet users who do not have home Internet access has almost halved, from 23 per cent in the eight months to February 2002, to 12 per cent  by January to April 2006. There are a number of other locations where people can access the Internet. In January to April 2006 the two most common places for adult Internet users without household access to go online were at work (46 per cent) and at another person's home (also 46 per cent) (Figure 2.2).

### Figure 2.2

**Where Internet users[1] go online other than at home, 2006[2]**

**Great Britain**
Percentages

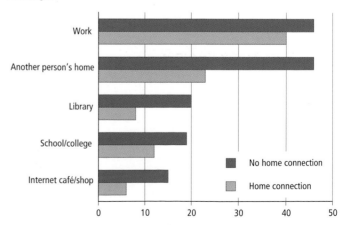

1  Adults aged 16 and over.
2  Data collected in January, February and April 2006.

*Source: Omnibus Survey, Office for National Statistics*

Data on Internet access in Northern Ireland collected in the Continuous Household Survey in 2005–06 indicated that more than one-half of all adults aged 16 and over in Northern Ireland (54 per cent) accessed the Internet, primarily through a computer at home (70 per cent). A lower proportion, 23 per cent, accessed the Internet through a computer at work, 3 per cent did so through a computer at their local library and 1 per cent went online using their mobile phone.

In 2000 the Government set a target of ensuring universal Internet access across the UK for all those who wanted it by 2005. To achieve this, the Government provided Internet-connected computers in libraries and places of public education, (see also Chapter 3: Access to ICT in education). In January to April 2006, 15 per cent of adults who were current Internet users went online in a place of education, 10 per cent in a public library, and 8 per cent in an Internet café. Current Internet users aged between 16 and 30 were more likely than current Internet users in other age groups to go online at another person's home, a place of education, a public library, or an Internet café.

In January to April 2006, 34 per cent of adults who were current Internet users had gone online in two different locations and 27 per cent had accessed the Internet in three or more locations. The number of locations where people access the Internet increases with the frequency that they use it. Nearly three-quarters (74 per cent) of current Internet users who went online every day used the Internet in more than one location compared with less than one-third (30 per cent) of those who went online once a month.

The majority of Internet users go online regularly. In January to April 2006, 59 per cent of current Internet users in Great Britain had gone online every day or almost every day, while 4 per cent went online less than once a month. Almost one-half of current Internet users in Northern Ireland (44 per cent) went online at least once a day, and more than one-quarter (28 per cent) went online several times a week.

## Connecting to the Internet

There are two main types of Internet connections: narrowband (dial-up) and broadband. On narrowband, the computer uses the telephone line to dial up for an Internet connection. Because narrowband access uses normal telephone lines, the quality of the connection can vary and data rates are limited. A narrowband user cannot be online and use the telephone at the same time.

Broadband has several advantages over narrowband, although the precise nature of the service offered varies by the Internet service provider (ISP). A provider may also offer more than one

type of broadband service. A broadband connection provides faster data transferral. This means that moving from one web-page to another or downloading large amounts of information, such as software, music or games, takes less time. It is also useful when the user has a particular need for quick communication or is engaged in real-time communication, for example, using web-radio or a chat room connection. A broadband connection allows users to use the telephone while online.

There are several ways that a broadband connection can be delivered. The two most common methods are through cable or a digital subscriber line (DSL). Cable modems deliver an Internet connection through the same cables that deliver cable television, whereas a DSL line uses normal telephone lines. In June 2003 DSL connections overtook cable modems as the dominant technology in the UK.

The proportion of households in Great Britain with any Internet connection increased from 50 per cent in 2003/04 to 57 per cent in January to April 2006 (Figure 2.3). During this period there was a trend towards greater use of broadband. The proportion of households with narrowband Internet access fell from 38 per cent in 2003/04 to 17 per cent in January to April 2006 while the proportion with broadband rose from 11 per cent to 40 per cent.

In January to April 2006, 62 per cent of people who lived in a household with home broadband access used the Internet every day or almost every day compared with 35 per cent who lived in a household with narrowband access and 6 per cent of those with no home access.

## Figure **2.3**

### Household Internet connection:¹ by type

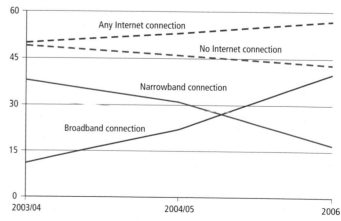

1 Data for 2003/04 and 2004/05 were collected in April (May in 2005), July, October and February. Data for 2006 were collected in January, February and April.

*Source: Omnibus Survey, Office for National Statistics*

The proportion of Internet users who have substantial Internet experience has steadily grown. In 2001/02, 42 per cent of Internet users aged 16 and over had more than three years' Internet experience. By 2004/05[3] this had increased to 65 per cent.

Between 2003/04 to 2005/06 more than one-half of adults (52 per cent) had home Internet access. Home access was highest in London (58 per cent of households) and the South East (57 per cent), and lowest in the North East and Wales, at 44 per cent and 45 per cent of households respectively (Table 2.4). One reason for the variation could be differences in household incomes across the regions. Between 2003/04 and 2005/06, average gross household income was highest in London, at £766 a week, followed by £687 a week in the South East. The lowest average gross household incomes were £455 a week in the North East and £492 in Wales. Across the UK average gross weekly household income was £596.

In January to April 2006 the regions with the highest proportion of the adult population who were current Internet users were the South East (67 per cent), and the East of England and London (both 65 per cent) (Table 2.5). The South West had the greatest proportion of adults who were current Internet users who had ever shopped online, at 79 per cent, followed by the East of England (77 per cent). London had the highest proportion of people in employment using the Internet

## Table 2.4

### Home Internet access and average household income

United Kingdom, 2003/04–2005/06[1]

|  | Homes with Internet access (Percentages) | Average gross weekly household income (£) |
|---|---|---|
| **United Kingdom** | 52 | 596 |
| **England** | 53 | 610 |
| North East | 44 | 455 |
| North West | 49 | 539 |
| Yorkshire and the Humber | 47 | 529 |
| East Midlands | 52 | 564 |
| West Midlands | 50 | 563 |
| East | 55 | 652 |
| London | 58 | 766 |
| South East | 57 | 687 |
| South West | 55 | 568 |
| **Wales** | 45 | 492 |
| **Scotland** | 49 | 544 |
| **Northern Ireland** | 41 | 498 |

1  Combined data from the 2003/04, 2004/05 and 2005/06 Expenditure and Food Surveys.

*Source: Expenditure and Food Survey, Office for National Statistics*

## Table 2.5

### Indicators of current Internet use[1]

Great Britain, 2006[2]

Percentages

|  | Adults who currently use the Internet | Go online at work[3] | Ever shopped online[4] | Go online at least five days a week[4] |
|---|---|---|---|---|
| **England** | 61 | 50 | 72 | 60 |
| North East | 62 | 45 | 68 | 55 |
| North West | 54 | 47 | 65 | 48 |
| Yorkshire and the Humber | 55 | 48 | 76 | 58 |
| East Midlands | 57 | 43 | 74 | 60 |
| West Midlands | 60 | 48 | 64 | 50 |
| East | 65 | 49 | 77 | 63 |
| London | 65 | 61 | 69 | 71 |
| South East | 67 | 49 | 75 | 60 |
| South West | 60 | 48 | 79 | 65 |
| **Scotland** | 48 | 35 | 68 | 58 |
| **Wales** | 52 | 33 | 71 | 53 |

1  Current users are defined as adults aged 16 and over who have used the Internet in the three months before interview.
2  Data collected in January, February and April 2006.
3  Percentage of people in employment who go online at work.
4  Percentage of current Internet users in the region.

*Source: Omnibus Survey, Office for National Statistics*

at work (61 per cent) and the highest proportion of current Internet users who went online at least five days in a typical week, at 71 per cent. Conversely adults in Scotland were less likely than those in other parts of the UK to be current Internet users, at 48 per cent. People in employment in Wales and Scotland were the least likely in the UK to use the Internet at work, at 33 per cent and 35 per cent respectively, and current Internet users in the North West were least likely to go online at least five days in a typical week, at 48 per cent.

## Online activities

Internet users access the Internet for many reasons. There is a range of online activities: sending and receiving emails, browsing (moving from one web-page or data source to another) and looking for information, finding information about goods and services, shopping, banking online, visiting chat rooms, downloading games, music, and software, reading online news, and listening to the radio or watching television through the Internet.

Using the Internet to find out information about goods and services and email are the two most common activities carried out online. Email allows people to send information to specified individuals, groups of individuals, organisations, government or business, and consists of written messages and attachments. Electronically stored documents, pictures, music and video can all be attached to an email. Between January and April 2006, 85 per cent of current Internet users looked for information about goods and services on the Internet and 81 per cent sent or received emails (Figure 2.6).

Between 2003/04 and January to April 2006, there was an increase in the proportion of current Internet users across a range of activities. The largest increase was in the proportion of people selling goods and services, which more than doubled from 7 per cent to 18 per cent. The proportion of Internet users who had played or downloaded music went up from one-quarter (25 per cent) to one-third (33 per cent) and the proportion who had bought or ordered tickets, goods and services also rose by 8 percentage points, from 50 per cent to 58 per cent over the same period.

### e-Shopping

In January to April 2006, 44 per cent of the adult population and 72 per cent of current Internet users in Great Britain said they had ever purchased something online for private or personal reasons other than work. The proportion of all adults who had shopped online in the three months before interview has increased. In 2001/02, 6 per cent of all adults had spent up to £100 online in the previous three months. By January to April 2006, this had increased to 11 per cent. Those spending

## Figure **2.6**

### Internet use:[1,2] by online activities

**Great Britain**
Percentages

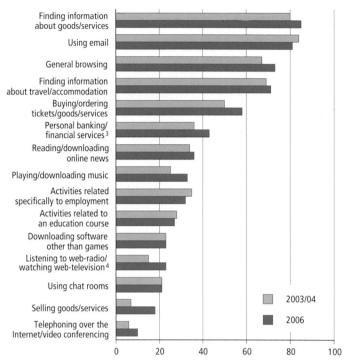

1  Adults aged 16 and over who used the Internet in the three months before interview.
2  Data for 2003/04 were collected in April, July, October and February. Data for 2006 were collected in January, February and April.
3  Internet banking only in 2003/04.
4  Listening to web-radio only in 2003/04.

*Source: Omnibus Survey, Office for National Statistics*

between £101 and £200 also increased over the same period, from 3 per cent to 7 per cent, while those spending between £201 and £500 and those spending more than £500 both rose from 3 per cent to 8 per cent.

In January to April 2006 current Internet users aged between 31 and 49 were more likely than those in other adult age groups to shop online, 65 per cent of Internet users of this age group had done so (Figure 2.7). People in this age group were also more likely than other age groups to spend £200 or more when shopping online. A greater proportion of graduate Internet users than non-graduates had shopped online, 76 per cent compared with 52 per cent, and had spent more than £200 online, 41 per cent compared with 23 per cent. Internet users in managerial or professional occupations were also more likely to shop online than those in other occupational categories, 70 per cent compared with 48 per cent. In addition, a greater proportion of male Internet users than female internet users had shopped online, 62 per cent compared with 54 per cent. See also 'Profile of Internet users' later in the chapter.

## Figure **2.7**

### Current Internet users[1] who shop online: by selected demographic characteristics, 2006[2]

**Great Britain**

Percentages

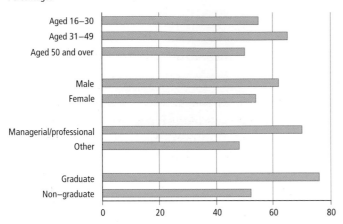

1  Adults aged 16 and over, who have used the Internet in the three months before interview.
2  Data collected in January, February and April 2006.

*Source: Omnibus Survey, Office for National Statistics*

The most common items bought online in the 12 months before interview in January to April 2006 were travel and holidays, at 51 per cent (Figure 2.8). Films, videos or DVDs were the next most common items purchased (42 per cent) and music or CDs (41 per cent). There was a difference between the kinds of goods and services that men and women purchased online. Men were more likely than women to buy videos or

## Figure **2.8**

### Internet shoppers: by items purchased[1,2]

**Great Britain**

Percentages

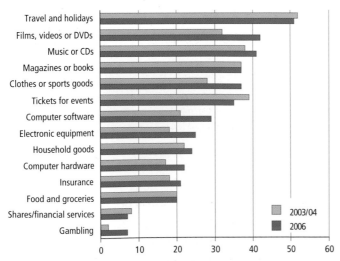

1  In the previous 12 months.
2  Data for 2003/04 were collected in April, July, October and February. Data for 2006 were collected in January, February and April.

*Source: Omnibus Survey, Office for National Statistics*

DVDs, music or CDs, computer software and hardware, and electronic equipment online, while women were more likely to buy clothes or sports goods, and food and groceries.

In January to April 2006 the Omnibus Survey found that 70 per cent of people who had shopped online within the last 12 months had not encountered any problems doing so. For those who had, the most common problem was that delivery took longer than indicated, which was experienced by 14 per cent of online shoppers. This was followed by the wrong goods being delivered, experienced by 6 per cent of online shoppers, and damaged goods being delivered, also experienced by 6 per cent.

Among Internet users who did not shop online, 42 per cent said that they preferred to shop in person or liked to see the product, and 37 per cent saw no need to shop online. More than one-third (35 per cent) were worried about security and this stopped them from shopping online.

Retailing online and traditional retail can be complementary, with companies maintaining established offline stores as well as an online presence. In January to April 2006 more than one-fifth of online shoppers (22 per cent) in Great Britain purchased only from online retailers they had known or found on the Internet. Just less than one-fifth (19 per cent) only purchased from online retailers they knew previously offline. More than one-half of online shoppers (57 per cent) purchased from both. Some Internet users research a prospective purchase online, but make the transaction in a traditional offline store. Conversely some will look at the goods in the store and then purchase online.

## Profile of Internet users

Children and young people in the UK are more likely than older people to be Internet users. Government policy[4] has been to provide all schools with Internet access, see also Chapter 3 e-education and e-skills.

Across the UK there have also been improved opportunities for children to access the Internet at home. In 2005/06, 72 per cent of households with one or more dependent child in the UK had Internet access compared with 47 per cent of households without a dependent child (Figure 2.9). In 1999–2000, 28 per cent of households with one or more dependent child had Internet access compared with 15 per cent of households without a dependent child.

The proportion of adults who use the Internet declines with age. In January to April 2006, 84 per cent of young people aged between 16 and 24 in Great Britain were current Internet users compared with 52 per cent of people aged between 55 and 64

## Figure **2.9**

### Household Internet access: by dependent child[1] living in the household

**United Kingdom**

Percentages

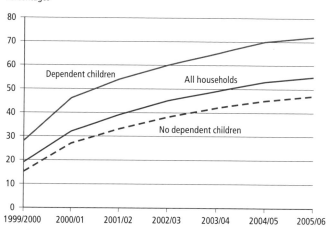

1 A dependent child is defined as a person aged 0–15 in a household or aged 16–17 in full-time education and who is not married.

*Source: Expenditure and Food Survey (from 2001/02 onwards) and Family Expenditure Survey (before 2001/02), Office for National Statistics*

and 15 per cent of those aged 65 and over (Figure 2.10). Between 2001/02 and January to April 2006, the proportion of Internet users grew in all age groups. The greatest increase was in the 55 to 64 age group, where the proportion of Internet users increased from 30 per cent in 2001/02 to 52 per cent by January to April 2006.

## Figure **2.10**

### Adults who currently[1,2] use the Internet: by age

**Great Britain**

Percentages

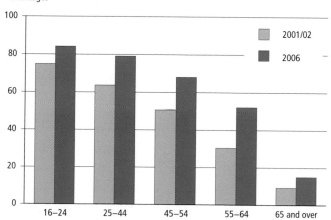

1 Current Internet users are defined as those who have gone online in the last three months.
2 Data for 2001/02 were collected in April, July, October and February. Data for 2006 were collected in January, February and April.
*Source: Omnibus Survey, Office for National Statistics*

In January to April 2006 the majority (81 per cent) of Internet users in the 16 to 24 age group in Great Britain lived in a household with Internet access. Among those aged 65 and over, 15 per cent used the Internet although 26 per cent lived in a household with Internet access. Similarly, in Northern Ireland 82 per cent of young people aged between 16 and 19 and 65 per cent of those aged 20 to 29 had Internet access at home in 2005–06, compared with 34 per cent of people aged 60 to 69 and 9 per cent of those aged 70 and over.

People with educational qualifications in Great Britain are more likely to use the Internet than those without (Figure 2.11). In January to April 2006, 88 per cent of people with a degree or higher qualification were current Internet users, four times the proportion of adults with no qualifications (22 per cent). Between 2001/02 and January to April 2006 growth in current Internet use was greatest among those with other qualifications below degree level, increasing from 58 per cent to 72 per cent.

## Figure **2.11**

### Adults who currently use the Internet:[1] by educational qualification

**Great Britain**

Percentages

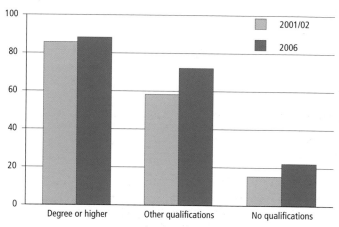

1 Adults aged 16 and over. Current Internet users are defined as those who have gone online in the last three months.
2 Data for 2001/02 were collected in April, July, October and February. Data for 2006 were collected in January, February and April

*Source: Omnibus Survey, Office for National Statistics*

Men are more likely to use the Internet than women. In January to April 2006, 65 per cent of men in Great Britain were current Internet users compared with 55 per cent of women. For men and women in employment percentages of current Internet users were roughly the same, 80 and 77 per cent respectively. Among people who are not in employment, a lower proportion of women than men were current Internet users, 35 per cent compared with 43 per cent.

Table **2.12**

**Reasons why individuals[1] do not use the Internet: by age**

Great Britain, 2004/05

Percentages

| | 16–49 | 50–74 | 75 and over | All non-users |
|---|---|---|---|---|
| Don't want/ need/have interest in | 30 | 48 | 58 | 46 |
| No connection | 41 | 38 | 42 | 40 |
| Lack knowledge or confidence | 37 | 35 | 33 | 36 |
| Internet offers no benefits | 9 | 12 | 16 | 12 |
| Cost is too high | 16 | 9 | 7 | 10 |
| Someone else uses it for me | 9 | 14 | 6 | 11 |
| Concerned about material available | 6 | 6 | 4 | 5 |

1 Adults aged 16 and over who do not use the Internet.

*Source: Omnibus Survey, Office for National Statistics*

## Profile of non-users of the Internet

The last time the Omnibus Survey asked non-users why they did not want to use the Internet was in 2004/05. In Great Britain, 30 per cent of non-users aged between 16 and 49 did not want, need or have interest in the Internet (Table 2.12). This increased to 48 per cent of non-users aged between 50 and 74 and to 58 per cent of those aged 75 and over. Around 40 per cent of non-users did not use the Internet because they didn't have a connection and 36 per cent lacked the knowledge and confidence to do so (see Chapter 3: e-Education and e-Skills).

Lack of interest and having no computer at home were also the most common reasons for adults not using the Internet in Northern Ireland, 46 per cent and 34 per cent respectively in 2005–06 (Table 2.13). Over one-half (54 per cent) of people of retirement age gave lack of interest as their most common reason for not using the Internet, as did nearly four

Table **2.13**

**Top five reasons for adults not using the Internet: by working age and retirement age[1]**

Northern Ireland, 2005–06

Percentages[2]

| | Working age | State Retirement age | All age groups |
|---|---|---|---|
| Lack of interest | 39 | 54 | 46 |
| No computer at home | 34 | 35 | 34 |
| Feel too old | 3 | 34 | 16 |
| Lack of confidence or skill | 10 | 13 | 11 |
| No need | 10 | 14 | 11 |

1 Working age is 16 to 59 for women and 16 to 64 for men. Retirement age is 60 for women and 65 for men.
2 Percentages do not add up to 100 as respondents could give more than one reason.

*Source: Continuous Household Survey, Northern Ireland Statistics and Research Agency*

in ten (39 per cent) of people of working age. More than one-third of people of retirement age (34 per cent) felt too old to use the Internet, while 11 per cent of all adults lacked confidence or skills.

One reason why adults do not use the Internet is that someone else does so for them. In 2004/05, 11 per cent of non-users in Great Britain had not used the Internet personally because someone else had gone online on their behalf. Indirect Internet use of this kind narrows the gap between Internet users and non-users, because the benefits of going online are spread more widely than among Internet users alone. However, both users and non-users ask others to go online on their behalf. In October 2003 (when users were last asked how frequently they had asked someone else to go online on their behalf) users did so more frequently than non-users, with 49 per cent of users asking someone else to get information online, shop online or send an email on their behalf, compared with 29 per cent of non-users and past users.

## Notes and references

1 Data were collected in January, February and April.

2 The question 'What equipment does your household have in order to access the Internet from home?' was last asked in the 2004/05 Omnibus Survey.

3 The question 'When did you first use the Internet?' was last asked in the 2004/05 Omnibus Survey.

4 In November 1998 the Government published the *Open for business, open for learning* challenge document, which included a target that all schools should have Internet access through the National Grid for Learning by 2002. Published by the British Educational Communications and Technology Agency (BECTa) for more information see www.becta.org.uk/careersict/publications

# e-Education and e-Skills

**Rachel Barker**
Department for Education and Skills
**Joe Gardiner**
Department of Trade and Industry

Chapter 3

## Introduction

As digital technology becomes more and more widespread, greater numbers of people need the skills and confidence to be able to use it effectively in their work and at home. In addition, there is an increasing demand for people with specialist skills to support the development of the information and communication technology (ICT) industries, and for people to unite e-skills with other professional skills so that ICT can be used to the best effect in industry and the professions.

## e-Learning

e-Learning is any learning using digital technology. It could include acquiring skills to use ICT, providing courses online and using ICT as a teaching aid. For example, a learner could use the Internet for research purposes, a data logger to record results from experiments in the field, an online forum to discuss a piece of coursework and a CD-ROM to get training, while a teacher could use an interactive whiteboard during a lesson.

In education ICT is seen as a means of transforming teaching and learning, and helping to break down barriers to educational achievement, particularly for those who struggle with traditional forms of learning. It provides a way of making information about education more accessible to parents and employers, as well as to learners. It also enables ideas and good practice to be shared between education providers and provides the flexibility of remote 'anytime, anywhere' learning.

## Access to ICT in education

Since 1998 ICT equipment levels have increased in all areas of education, with significantly improved computer-to-learner ratios, Internet connection speeds and networking. Between 1998 and 2004 computer-to-pupil ratios in England improved from 17.6 to 7.5 pupils per computer in primary schools and from 8.7 to 4.9 pupils per computer in secondary schools (Figure 3.1). In special schools, where levels of ICT provision have traditionally been higher, the ratio fell from 4.5 to 3.0 pupils per computer.

There was a similar picture in further education colleges, where the average number of full-time equivalent (FTE) students per computer in England improved from 8.2 students per computer in 1999 to 4.8 in 2005.

In higher education the number of FTE students per computer in Great Britain reported in the Higher Education Information Technology Statistics[1] was higher, at 7.8 in 2005, although this ratio had fallen from 10.8 students per computer in 1999. There was an increasing trend for network access in halls of residence, with network access points reported in 75 per cent of rooms.

Figure **3.1**

**Number of pupils per computer:[1] by type of school**

England

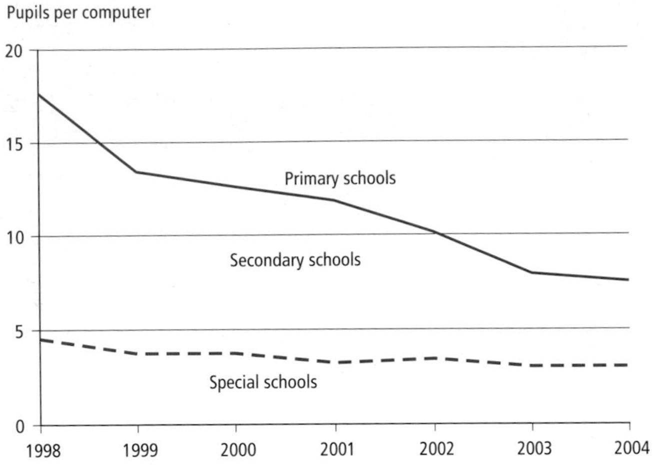

Pupils per computer

1 Computers mainly used for teaching and learning in full-time education.

*Source: ICT in Schools Survey, Department for Education and Skills/British Educational Communications and Technology Agency*

By 2004 all universities and colleges in the UK had broadband access to the Internet, and broadband access for schools had increased. Between 2002 and 2004 the proportion of secondary schools with broadband access in England went up from 68 per cent to 90 per cent; for primary schools it increased from 11 per cent to 30 per cent; and for special schools, from 11 per cent to 40 per cent.

However, rising levels of equipment do not necessarily mean that the available levels of equipment and access are sufficient. The British Educational Communications and Technology Agency (Becta) Survey of ICT in Further Education in England[2] found that despite rising levels of infrastructure provision the number of colleges stating they had difficulty meeting demand had risen in recent years, from 28 per cent in 2001 to 40 per cent in 2005. While this change may be partly attributable to random effects, for example different colleges responding in different years, it seems probable that it is also because demand is rising as student numbers and levels of use increase.

In the 2002 report *ICT in Schools* the Office for Standards in Education in England (Ofsted) found that there was a great willingness to use ICT in teaching and learning within schools. This was reflected in colleges too. The 2004 ICT in Schools Survey[3] found that most (more than 90 per cent) had a strategy for implementing and reviewing the use of ICT. Further education colleges are required by their funding body to have an ICT strategy. In the workplace, government policy is directed at raising awareness of the potential of e-learning to assist in developing skills and improving business performance.

## Staff skills in ICT

To make effective use of ICT in teaching and learning, staff must possess the necessary skills. Responses to the 2004 ICT in Schools Survey showed that in the majority of schools in England teachers had received appropriate levels of training and guidance on the use of ICT and that most of the staff were confident users of ICT: 85 per cent in primary schools, 81 per cent in secondary schools, and 86 per cent in special schools (Figure 3.2). These proportions had gone up from 65 per cent, 61 per cent and 63 per cent respectively in 1998.

### Figure **3.2**

### Staff confident in the use of ICT in their subject teaching: by type of school

England

Percentages

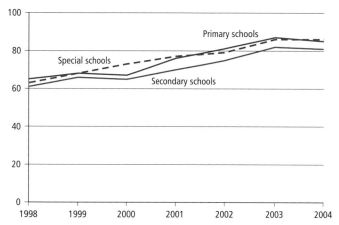

Source: ICT in Schools Survey, Department for Education and Skills/British Educational Communications and Technology Agency

The Survey of ICT in Further Education in England approach was slightly different to the ICT in Schools Survey and looked at competence rather than confidence. It distinguished between personal competence in the use of ICT and competence in the use of ICT specifically for teaching and learning. On average colleges in England in 2005 estimated that while 77 per cent of their staff were competent in their personal use of ICT, 59 per cent were competent in the use of ICT for teaching and learning purposes. This highlights a concern in education that simply being able to use the technology is not enough; while good e-skills are a prerequisite for effective e-teaching it does not follow that those who know how to use ICT also know how to teach well with it.

The above results came from responses from the organisation as opposed to the individual teachers. A lack of a commonly agreed and well understood set of definitions of ICT competences, taken with uncertainty about what constitutes good practice and effective e-teaching, may have led respondents to overstate the ICT skill level of staff or to reach different conclusions as to how well ICT was used in teaching.

## ICT use by teachers and learners

A majority of school teachers are reported to make regular use of ICT in teaching and learning. This varies by type of school, with primary and special school teachers in England, 92 and 91 per cent respectively in 2004, more likely to use ICT than secondary teachers, 70 per cent.

Use levels varied across the curriculum, with ICT as a course subject inevitably the highest, 84 per cent of primary school responses, 99 per cent of secondary school and 87 per cent of special school responses (Figure 3.3). After ICT as a subject, the next highest use of ICT in primary schools was in English lessons, 63 per cent, followed by mathematics, 56 per cent. In secondary schools, less use appeared to be made of ICT in these subject areas, 24 per cent and 41 per cent of responses reporting substantial use respectively for English and mathematics. Greater use was reported for design and technology, 66 per cent. With the exception of ICT as a subject and English taught in special schools, use levels had grown in all areas of the curriculum since 2002. An increasing range of ICT equipment was also in use with growing numbers of schools using interactive whiteboards and digital (data) projectors.

As part of the Survey of ICT in Further Education, colleges in England were asked whether the particular use is employed in all, most, some, few or no programmes. Overall, the extent to which colleges use ICT within mainstream teaching and

### Figure **3.3**

### Use of ICT in areas of the curriculum: by type of school

England

Percentages

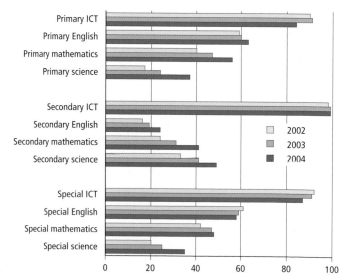

Source: ICT in Schools Survey, Department for Education and Skills/British Educational Communications and Technology Agency

learning activities increased between 2003 and 2004. However, this was followed in 2005 by a reduction of use of ICT in most areas (Figure 3.4). Only blended learning (a flexible combination of online and classroom learning activities) and remote learning showed further increases. The reasons for these changes in patterns of use are unclear, but may be partly because of changes in the way colleges define blended learning, with activities previously placed in other categories now seen as blended learning. Also e-learning is in the early stages of development, so many uses are experimental and may be used one year and dropped the next.

ICT is most commonly used to support learning, for example, using the Internet for research, or technology-based exercises

## Figure **3.4**

### Use of ICT in most or all college mainstream programmes

**England**

Percentages

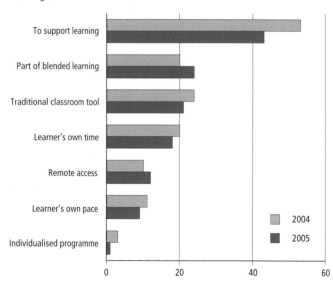

*Source: British Educational Communications and Technology Agency*

for revision or practice, with 43 per cent of colleges responding that they used it in all or most programmes in 2005. It was least frequently used for individualised learning programmes (1 per cent) and for learners to work at their own pace (9 per cent).

There is increasing use of a range of ICT in further education. Data projectors were used in 98 per cent of colleges in England in 2005 and virtual learning environments – technology that is used by teachers and learners to interact online in various ways – were used by around 76 per cent of colleges. Use of other ICT such as interactive whiteboards is also increasing, with a majority of colleges now having these available in at least some lecture rooms.

In the wider adult learning community the use of ICT for taught learning also appears to be increasing. In 2002 responses to the National Adult Learners Survey showed 49 per cent of taught learners in England had used ICT for their learning, an increase from 44 per cent in the previous year. In each case around one-half of those using a computer for their course said they used it most or all of the time. The most common use (34 per cent) was for word processing or using a spreadsheet, but a significant proportion (20 per cent) were taking courses in learning information technology (IT) skills (computer skills), and 16 per cent were using a computer to get information about their course (Figure 3.5). More than one-half, 51 per cent, did not use a computer for the course.

## Figure **3.5**

### Use of ICT by adult learners for taught learning, 2002

**England**

Percentages

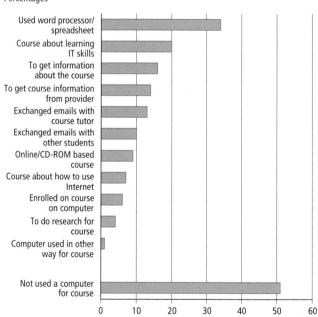

*Source: National Adult Learners Survey, Department for Education and Skills*

The proportions using ICT for self-directed learning were higher, with 61 per cent who reported self-directed learning in 2002 saying they had used ICT, a similar proportion to 2001 (60 per cent). The most common use was for research connected with learning (46 per cent). As with taught learning, around one-half of those using ICT for learning did so most or all of the time. It is likely that some of the e-learning done by adults was in connection with work, or in the workplace.

## Impact of ICT in education

The use of ICT in education can have an impact in a number of ways:

- on learning outcomes, such as exam performance and employability

- on intermediate learning outcomes such as learner motivation, engagement and independence

- on non-learning outcomes such as management efficiency and workload reduction

This section looks at each in turn.

There has been keen interest in whether the use of ICT for teaching and learning has an effect on student attainment. Analysis of Key Stage test results and Office for Standards in Education in England (Ofsted) data on the availability of good ICT learning opportunities and resources showed that in primary schools that had full Ofsted inspections in 2002, Key Stage 2 test results were higher in schools where Ofsted judged ICT resources to be good than in those where they were judged to be poor. This was the case even where schools were similar in terms of socio-economic characteristics and overall quality of management. However, these findings should be qualified as a number of successful schools (those where previous inspections were good, exam and test results were good compared with national standards and to similar schools, and where trends were positive) that had short inspections were excluded from the sample. It is not known whether the findings would apply equally to these more successful schools.

There has also been interest as to whether the availability of a computer in the home can make a difference to achievement. Research for the Centre for Economic Performance published in 2004 showed that in Great Britain, where there was a computer in the home, pupils were more likely to obtain more than five GCSEs and to gain at least one A level.[4] This was true even when household wealth and income were taken into account. However, a crucial factor appears to be the type of computer use. In particular, there seems to be a growing body of evidence to suggest that use of the computer for educational purposes is positively linked, but extensive use for entertainment purposes is negatively linked with attainment.

Influences on academic attainment, which include teacher style and competence, school and academic leadership, and the characteristics of the learner, are complex. There is insufficient understanding of the impact of ICT on people's abilities and understanding to claim categorically that using a computer improves academic attainment. It is not certain whether the effects of using a computer are largely superficial, allowing students to improve the presentation of their work to gain a few extra marks, for instance, or whether there are more fundamental effects on improving knowledge and understanding of a subject.

One area where ICT is perceived to have an important influence is on learner motivation. A study of pupils and teachers in 17 primary and secondary schools in England in 2004[5] found that ICT use had a positive effect on motivation across the age ranges for both boys and girls. This was shown in a variety of ways, including improvements in behaviour in school and completion of homework. In particular ICT was found to help motivate and engage pupils with disabilities, and those who were disaffected with traditional forms of learning. ICT was also perceived to have a positive impact on helping children with special educational needs (SEN) in the 2004 ICT in Schools Survey. A majority (71 per cent) of special schools in England reported that ICT had a substantial impact on helping pupils with SEN. While this was much lower for both primary schools (19 per cent) and secondary schools (30 per cent), few schools (8 per cent of primary, 5 per cent of secondary and 1 per cent of special schools) reported no impact.

The ability of ICT to improve administrative effectiveness and efficiency is difficult to measure. A study on the effect of ICT on teacher workload in England in 2004 found that where ICT was effectively used, it could reduce the time spent on tasks, but that good organisational leadership, appropriate training, technical support and effective ICT networks were all prerequisites for this to happen.[6] Failure to provide these prerequisites could result in a lack of IT skills and confidence on the part of staff and actually increase the time taken to complete tasks using ICT.

In the ICT in Schools Survey, the majority of schools reported some reduction in workload attributable to the use of ICT for administration and management, while 10 per cent of special schools, 9 per cent of primary schools and 7 per cent of secondary schools reported a substantial reduction. However, around 10 per cent of schools in each sector reported an increase in teacher workloads as a result of ICT.

Although there has been considerable development, there is much variation in the adoption, use and impact of ICT within the education sector. The search for a general picture of progress has led to the development of concepts of 'embeddedness' – that is the degree to which ICT is firmly fixed in teaching and learning across the curriculum – and 'e-confidence'.

There have been several attempts at classifying these concepts. Most models identify a minority of schools or colleges as innovators, with ICT widely adopted and understood across the organisation, and a minority struggling to make headway or resisting the adoption of ICT. The majority of institutions have some understanding of the importance of ICT and, although they have made some progress towards tapping that potential, realise they have some way to go to integrate e-learning fully into mainstream teaching and learning.

## General user skills

Use of ICT in education may make people more employable by equipping them with ICT skills. There is a distinction between general ICT user skills, such as the ability to use word processors, email and general office software, and specialist ICT skills such as programming and systems analysis, which are required to support the IT and media industries.

Many people obtain their computer skills from more than one source. The ONS Omnibus Survey 2006 found that the most common ways that adults in the UK acquired ICT skills were learning-by-doing (48 per cent) and receiving informal assistance from colleagues, friends and family (45 per cent) (Table 3.6). Nearly one-third (30 per cent) obtained their ICT skills in a formal educational institution such as a school or college.

While increasing numbers of people are using ICT, their skill levels are often not well developed. The Skills for Life Survey in England in 2003,[7] which sought to measure people's ability to use ICT, found that while awareness of ICT was quite advanced, the ability to manipulate it was much less so. Measuring people's abilities against prototype standards for ICT awareness and practical skills, where entry level was the most basic level, and level 1, level 2 and higher levels represented gradually increasing skills, the Survey found that while 75 per cent of respondents had awareness above entry level, less than 50 per cent had practical skills at entry level 2 or above.

Skill levels were closely related to how often people used computers, with frequent users demonstrating higher levels of

## Table **3.6**

### Where and how adults obtained ICT skills, 2006

| United Kingdom | Percentages |
| --- | --- |
| Self-study in the sense of learning-by-doing | 48 |
| Informal assistance from colleagues, relatives, friends | 45 |
| Formal educational institution (school, college, university, etc) | 30 |
| Vocational training courses (on the demand of employer) | 24 |
| Self-study using books, cd-roms, etc | 17 |
| Training courses in adult education centre (but not on employer's initiative) | 15 |
| Some other way | 1 |

*Source: Omnibus Survey, Office for National Statistics*

skill. They were also related to occupational level, with 77 per cent of those in managerial and professional occupations achieving the highest levels of awareness and practical skills, compared with 44 per cent of those in work overall and 12 per cent of those in routine occupations. This occupational effect persisted even for those who were frequent users, with 82 per cent of frequent users in higher professional and managerial occupations achieving the highest test scores compared with 31 per cent of frequent users working in routine occupations.

## Specialist ICT skills

In 2002, 8,300 new graduates entered the ICT workforce in the UK as their first employment, almost one-half from computer science disciplines.[8] Those studying IT courses in higher education have steadily declined from a peak in 2000.

In further education, skills development is provided for both IT users (mainly at levels 1 and 2) and IT professionals (mainly level 3). In 2003, 416,000 IT user courses and 46,000 IT professional qualifications were completed in the UK. Employers are increasingly seeking higher level skills and, supported by e-skills UK (the sector skills council for the ICT sector), are improving their links with educators to help to meet this challenge.

Overall the employment of ICT staff in the UK showed a small rise during 2004, with approximately 961,000 people employed as ICT professional staff at the end of the year. This was a slight fall from 2001 levels, when nearly 1 million people were employed as ICT professionals. The general trends from 2001 to 2004 were a rise during 2001, a fall during 2002, and a recovery during 2003 and 2004. e-skills UK reported that the upturn in the ICT labour market continued during the final quarter of 2004 with increased demand for ICT staff across all recruitment channels.

e-Skills UK forecast in 2004 that the IT workforce will grow at between 1.5 per cent and 2.2 per cent a year over the ten years to 2015. Similarly, the IT industry, driven by IT services, is forecast to grow by between 2 per cent and 3 per cent over the same period.[8] The roles of IT professionals are changing, with an increased need for broadly based interpersonal and project skills as well as technical skills.

The incidence of professional skills shortages in the ICT sector is much lower than those of IT user skills gaps. In an employer survey by e-skills UK, 95 per cent of establishments reported ICT professional skills gaps and 13 per cent reported IT user skills gaps. These mainly related to keeping up to date with new technologies for IT professionals, and the requirement for continued development of office application skills for IT users.

Computer education in schools is improving the IT literacy of the future UK workforce. However, this is mainly addressing basic IT user skills needs rather than skills in the strategic use of IT and professional IT skills. Employer training and private training are the major providers for IT skills development post-education in the UK.

## Notes and references

1    The Higher Education Information Technology Statistics (HEITS) have been published annually since 1997 by the Universities and Colleges Information Systems Association (UCISA). www.ucisa.ac.uk/activities/stats/

2    The Survey of ICT in Further Education was carried out in England by the British Educational Communications and Technology Agency (Becta) on behalf of the Learning and Skills Council. It identified a number of different teaching and learning activities following a model of e-learning developed by Jenny Scribbins and Bob Powell (a fuller exposition of this model can be found in *Managing inspection and ILT*, Becta 2003). There is no direct comparability with the ICT in Schools Survey as the questions were framed differently.

3    Prior G and Hall L (2004) *ICT in Schools Survey 2004*. Department for Education and Skills/Becta. The 2004 ICT in Schools Survey was carried out by the British Educational Communications and Technology Agency (Becta) on behalf of the Department for Education and Skills. The Survey covered provision and usage of ICT in maintained primary, secondary and special schools in England. It used a curriculum-based approach and was carried out annually between 1998 and 2004.

4    Schmitt J and Wadsworth J (2004) *Is There an Impact of Household Computer Ownership on Children's Educational Attainment in Britain?* Centre for Economic Performance (CEP) Discussion Paper No. 625.

5    Passey D, Rogers C, Machell J and McHugh G (2004) *The motivational effect of ICT on pupils*. Department for Education and Skills Research Report RR523.

6    PricewaterhouseCoopers (2004) *Moving towards e-learning in schools and FE colleges: models of resource planning at the institutional level*. Department for Education and Skills Research Report RR601.

7    Williams J, Clemens S, Oleinikova K and Tarvin K (2003) *The skills for life survey: a national needs and impact survey of literacy, numeracy and ICT skills*. Department for Education and Skills Research Report RR490.

8    e-skills UK/Gartner Consulting (2004) *IT Insights: Trends and UK Skills Implications*. e-skills UK is the skills council for the ICT sector.

# e-Business

**Chapter 4**

**Mark Pollard**
Office for National Statistics
**Lindsay Clothier**
Department for Environment,
Food and Rural Affairs

## Introduction

The rapid growth in business use of computers has often been the headline, but the story is more complicated than that. Considerable differences exist in the adoption and use of digital technology between businesses of different size and different economic activity. Typically the larger the business the more information and communication technology (ICT) is used. On the other hand in recent years the fastest growth in usage has been among smaller businesses, that is those with fewer than 50 employees,[1] as they 'catch-up' in their ICT use.

Much of the data used in this chapter are taken from the 2005 e-Commerce Survey, which is based on businesses with ten or more employees. Businesses with fewer than ten employees were excluded from the 2005 survey, although they were included in previous e-Commerce Surveys. This has an effect on the data because of the relatively low ICT activity among smaller businesses and the large number of small businesses.

For this reason businesses with fewer than ten employees have also been excluded from data from earlier e-Commerce Surveys, so that comparisons can be made.

## ICT use

There has been widespread adoption of some ICT by businesses of most sizes. In 2005, 93 per cent of businesses in the UK reported using personal computers or similar devices (Table 4.1), up from 89 per cent in 2002. Computer use is nearing saturation level by businesses with ten or more employees. Nearly 100 per cent of the largest businesses (those with 1,000 or more employees) and 100 per cent of businesses with between 250 and 999 employees used computers, while 92 per cent of businesses with between 10 and 49 employees did so.

Websites have become an essential means of communication with customers for many businesses (see also Chapter 5:

## Table 4.1

### Business use of ICT: by number of employees

**United Kingdom**  Percentages

| | 10–49 | 50–249 | 250–999 | 1,000 or more | All businesses with 10 or more |
|---|---|---|---|---|---|
| **Computers, workstations, terminals, etc** | | | | | |
| 2002 | 87.2 | 97.5 | 99.3 | 99.3 | 89.0 |
| 2003 | 90.6 | 98.6 | 99.3 | 99.5 | 92.1 |
| 2004 | 90.7 | 99.0 | 99.7 | 99.9 | 92.2 |
| 2005 | 92.0 | 98.9 | 100.0 | 99.6 | 93.3 |
| **With website, own or third party** | | | | | |
| 2002 | 53.9 | 77.0 | 88.1 | 95.1 | 58.3 |
| 2003 | 57.5 | 82.6 | 89.8 | 96.8 | 62.2 |
| 2004 | 62.7 | 84.9 | 92.4 | 97.9 | 66.9 |
| 2005 | 65.7 | 86.7 | 94.8 | 97.7 | 69.8 |
| **Intranet** | | | | | |
| 2002 | 19.4 | 44.1 | 65.0 | 82.0 | 24.5 |
| 2003 | 23.1 | 47.2 | 69.0 | 83.9 | 28.2 |
| 2004 | 24.9 | 45.3 | 69.2 | 84.6 | 29.4 |
| 2005 | 25.5 | 48.6 | 74.3 | 86.4 | 30.6 |
| **Extranet** | | | | | |
| 2002 | 3.7 | 9.6 | 23.4 | 35.4 | 5.2 |
| 2003 | 5.3 | 11.0 | 23.8 | 39.7 | 6.9 |
| 2004 | 4.5 | 13.5 | 26.7 | 41.4 | 6.6 |
| 2005 | 6.0 | 15.0 | 33.1 | 48.5 | 8.4 |

*Source: e-Commerce Survey, Office for National Statistics*

e-Commerce and ICT-equipped employees). In 2005, 70 per cent of businesses reported having a website, an increase from 58 per cent in 2002. Nearly nine in ten businesses with 50 to 249 employees (87 per cent) had a website at the end of 2005, compared with 98 per cent of businesses with 1,000 or more employees.

Just less than one-third (31 per cent) of businesses reported having an intranet in 2005, an increase from 25 per cent in 2002. While 86 per cent of businesses with 1,000 or more employees had an intranet, 25 per cent of businesses with between 10 and 49 employees had one. An intranet is a private network for internal use inside an organisation that uses the same kind of software that would also be found on the Internet.

A smaller proportion of businesses than those with an intranet reported having an extranet, 8 per cent in 2005. Just under one-half (49 per cent) of businesses with 1,000 or more employees had an extranet, compared with 6 per cent of those with between 10 and 49 employees. An extranet is part of a company's intranet that is extended to users outside the company, such as suppliers, customers, partners and other businesses.

Between 2003 and 2004 improved geographic coverage, aggressive marketing and competitive pricing resulted in a 42 per cent rise in businesses reporting broadband as their primary method for Internet connection, to 60 per cent. For the 2002, 2003 and 2004 e-Commerce Surveys, a broadband connection was defined as a cable/direct subscriber line (DSL), other fixed broadband or a satellite/wireless broadband connection. For the 2005 survey a broadband connection was defined as one where the connection speed is 144Kbps or more. In 2005, 75 per cent of businesses had a broadband Internet connection, a rise of 25 per cent on 2004 (Table 4.2). Generally the larger the business, the more likely it is to have broadband although growth is fastest in the smaller businesses as the larger businesses reach saturation point. The proportion of businesses with between 10 and 49 employees that had broadband was 38 per cent in 2003. By 2005 this had increased to 71 per cent. Growth was slower in the largest businesses with 1,000 or more employees, with increases of 8 per cent in 2004 to 94 per cent having broadband and of 5 per cent in 2005 to 99 per cent having broadband. Businesses with between 250 and 999 employees were also close to saturation, with 97 per cent having broadband, with businesses with 50 to 249 employees not far behind, at 92 per cent.

The Office for National Statistics (ONS) quarterly Index of Internet Connectivity in the UK presents evidence of continuing growth. In December 2005, 65 per cent of all connections (including households) were broadband connections, (see also Chapter 2 for household Internet use). In 2005, according to the e-Commerce Survey, 14 per cent of businesses had a fastest connection speed

## Table 4.2

### Businesses with Internet access: by number of employees, type of connection and maximum available speed

United Kingdom, 2005                                                                                                    Percentages

| | Number of employees | | | | All businesses with 10 or more |
|---|---|---|---|---|---|
| | 10–49 | 50–249 | 250–999 | 1,000 or more | |
| **Type of connection** | | | | | |
| Dial-up connection | 31.2 | 42.6 | 55.2 | 60.5 | 33.7 |
| ISDN[1] | 25.9 | 40.2 | 51.4 | 59.9 | 28.9 |
| DSL[2] | 64.6 | 79.8 | 82.0 | 86.0 | 67.4 |
| Other fixed Internet connection | 8.7 | 30.0 | 60.7 | 77.2 | 13.6 |
| Mobile Internet connection | 18.9 | 41.7 | 59.9 | 66.5 | 23.6 |
| **Maximum connection speed** | | | | | |
| Less than 144Kbps | 16.0 | 5.9 | 2.6 | 0.9 | 14.1 |
| 144Kbps or more, and less than 2Mbps | 47.5 | 45.0 | 31.4 | 20.4 | 46.5 |
| 2Mbps or more | 23.3 | 46.6 | 65.7 | 78.3 | 28.3 |

1  Integrated Services Digital Network.
2  Digital subscriber line.

*Source: e-Commerce Survey, Office for National Statistics*

that was less than 144Kbps (that is, a narrowband or dial-up connection) a fall of 37 per cent compared with 2004. This followed a fall of 24 per cent between 2003 and 2004 in the proportion of businesses with a narrowband connection, from 30 per cent of businesses with Internet access at the end of 2003 to 22 per cent at the end of 2004.

The type of connection through which businesses access the Internet varies and businesses may use more than one type of connection. In 2005, two-thirds (67 per cent) of businesses had direct subscriber line (DSL) connections, 34 per cent had dial-up, 29 per cent had ISDN[2] and 24 per cent had a mobile Internet connection.

## Selling and buying over the Internet

An increasing proportion of businesses are selling products or services over the Internet. In 2005, 15 per cent sold over the Internet compared with 7 per cent in 2002 (Table 4.3). A greater proportion of businesses also purchased over the Internet, 56 per cent in 2005, three times the proportion of 18 per cent in 2002. Nearly four times more businesses buy than sell over the Internet. A slightly larger proportion compared with selling over the Internet (17 per cent in 2005) sold products and services through other ICT (such as Electronic Data Exchange, email, computer-based faxes and automated telephone entry like the type used for ordering

## Table 4.3

### Businesses trading through electronic means: by number of employees

United Kingdom

Percentages

| | Number of employees | | | | All businesses with 10 or more |
|---|---|---|---|---|---|
| | 10–49 | 50–249 | 250–999 | 1,000 or more | |
| **Sold over the Internet** | | | | | |
| 2002 | 6.4 | 7.7 | 14.4 | 22.3 | 6.9 |
| 2003 | 9.1 | 10.6 | 16.0 | 27.4 | 9.6 |
| 2004 | 10.6 | 17.0 | 22.7 | 31.5 | 12.0 |
| 2005 | 12.9 | 20.9 | 28.5 | 38.6 | 14.6 |
| **Purchased over the Internet** | | | | | |
| 2002 | 15.8 | 23.7 | 31.0 | 37.3 | 17.5 |
| 2003 | 37.6 | 50.3 | 57.5 | 58.1 | 40.0 |
| 2004 | 47.7 | 61.9 | 64.9 | 69.2 | 50.3 |
| 2005 | 52.8 | 71.1 | 77.1 | 79.1 | 56.3 |
| **Sold over other ICT (excluding the Internet)[1]** | | | | | |
| 2002 | 9.2 | 20.4 | 33.9 | 30.2 | 11.5 |
| 2003 | 14.5 | 24.2 | 35.3 | 34.0 | 16.5 |
| 2004 | 13.2 | 24.9 | 33.2 | 34.8 | 15.6 |
| 2005 | 15.0 | 24.1 | 32.8 | 36.8 | 16.9 |
| **Purchased over other ICT (excluding the Internet)[1]** | | | | | |
| 2002 | 10.4 | 19.2 | 33.7 | 48.0 | 12.5 |
| 2003 | 15.8 | 24.5 | 43.9 | 57.7 | 18.0 |
| 2004 | 14.3 | 29.3 | 39.6 | 54.3 | 17.3 |
| 2005 | 16.0 | 26.9 | 42.6 | 56.3 | 18.5 |

1 Includes Electronic Data Interchange, email, computer-based fax and automated telephone entry.

*Source: e-Commerce Survey, Office for National Statistics*

cinema tickets). The proportion of businesses that purchased over other ICT was 18 per cent in 2005. Again larger businesses were more likely to buy and sell over the Internet and over other ICT, although the proportions increased for businesses of all sizes between 2002 and 2005.

Businesses in the post and telecommunications sector were the most likely to purchase over the Internet, 78 per cent did so in 2005. They were also the most likely to sell over the Internet, 23 per cent did so in 2005. The manufacturing sector was most likely to sell over other ICT excluding the Internet, at 29 per cent of businesses in this sector (see also Chapter 6: e-Commerce for international comparison).

## Selling over the Internet

In 2005 the value of sales over the Internet accounted for 34 per cent of sales over all kinds of ICT and 6 per cent of the total sales by the non-financial sectors. The rise, from £66.2 billion in 2004 to £103.3 billion in 2005, represented an increase of 56 per cent in the value of sales over the Internet compared with a rise of 22 per cent in the proportion of businesses reporting that they sell over the Internet. This continued the pattern seen in the data collected since 2002.

There remains a clear divide between the smallest and largest businesses. Nearly four in ten (39 per cent) businesses with 1,000 or more employees in the non-financial sector sold over the Internet in 2005, compared with more than one in ten (13 per cent) of the smaller businesses with between 10 and 49 employees.

Among non-financial sector businesses the largest relative increase year on year in Internet sales was among those with between 50 and 249 employees, where the value of sales over the Internet rose by 151 per cent from £7 billion in 2004 to £18 billion in 2005 (Figure 4.4). Businesses with 1,000 or more employees accounted for £48 of every £100 sold over the Internet in 2005. This compared with a fall in the share of Internet sales from £59 in every £100 sold over the Internet in 2003 and £55 of every £100 sold in 2004, reflecting the relatively larger increases in use of the Internet for selling by smaller businesses.

The wholesale, retail, catering and travel sector reported £49 billion of sales over the Internet in 2005, representing £47 of every £100 sold over the Internet. It also reported the largest year on year rise in the value of sales over the Internet, a rise of 71 per cent from £29 billion in 2004 (Figure 4.5). Although the post and telecommunications sector had the largest proportion of businesses selling over the Internet, sales by this sector were only £4.7 billion in 2005.

Figure **4.4**

**Value of sales over the Internet: by number of employees[1]**

United Kingdom

£ billion

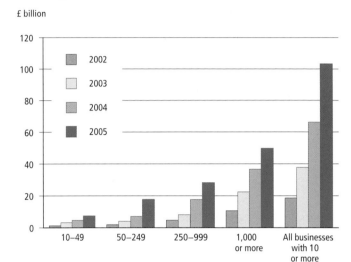

1   Non-financial sector businesses.

*Source: e-Commerce Survey, Office for National Statistics*

Figure **4.5**

**Value of sales over the Internet: by selected broad industrial sector[1]**

United Kingdom

£ billion

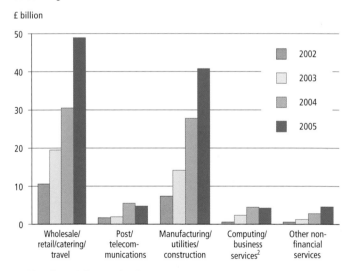

1   Non-financial sector businesses.
2   Includes renting and real estate.

*Source: e-Commerce Survey, Office for National Statistics*

While the proportion of businesses reporting that they had a website was nearly 70 per cent in 2005 (see Table 4.1), 15 per cent of businesses reported selling over the Internet in the same year. This suggests that the majority used their websites for purposes other than selling, such as product and company information.

## Buying over the Internet

In direct comparison to sales, nearly four times the proportion of businesses bought over the Internet, at least once, in 2005 – just over 56 per cent compared with nearly 15 per cent. More than half of businesses with ten or more employees reported some online purchases in 2005.

The value of purchases bought over the Internet has grown for all businesses with ten or more employees, and in total rose almost fivefold from £15 billion in 2002 to £73 billion in 2005. Between 2004 and 2005 the value of purchases rose by 50 per cent from the 2004 figure of £48 billion. Businesses with 1,000 or more employees spent £35 of every £100 spent buying over the Internet in 2005 (Figure 4.6). Smaller businesses with between 10 and 49 employees spent £17 of every £100 spent over the Internet. The largest percentage year on year increases were in businesses with 250 to 999 employees, with a 65 per cent growth in purchases over the Internet between 2004 and 2005. All other sizes of businesses with ten or more employees reported increases ranging from 44 per cent to 49 per cent.

All sectors of the economy showed a year on year increase in their purchases over the Internet between 2002 and 2005. The wholesale, retail, catering and travel sector had the largest online spend, £59 of every £100 of the £73 billion total in 2005 (Figure 4.7). The manufacturing sector spent nearly £22 of every £100 spent online, and was the second biggest online spender. The 'other (non-financial) services' sector showed the largest year on year increase, at 125 per cent between 2004 and 2005, although this was from a low base, of £1.2 billion in 2004 to £2.7 billion in 2005.

## Figure **4.6**

### Value of purchases bought over the Internet: by number of employees[1]

**United Kingdom**

£ billion

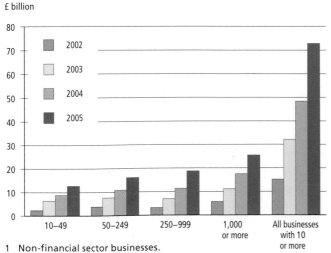

1  Non-financial sector businesses.

*Source: e-Commerce Survey, Office for National Statistics*

## Figure **4.7**

### Value of purchases bought over the Internet: by selected broad industrial sector[1]

**United Kingdom**

£ billion

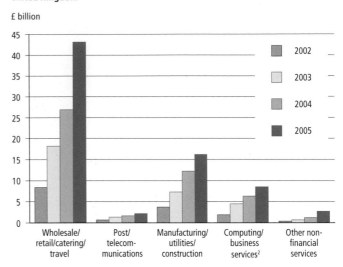

1  Non-financial sector businesses.
2  Includes renting and real estate.

*Source: e-Commerce Survey, Office for National Statistics*

## Buying and selling over non-Internet ICT

The value of sales over the Internet rose by 56 per cent between 2004 and 2005, from £66 billion to £103 billion, while the value of sales made over other ICT (such as Electronic Data Interchange over non-Internet systems, email, computer-based fax and automated telephone entry) increased by 12 per cent, from £183 billion to £204 billion.

In 2005 businesses sold almost twice as much using forms of ICT other than the Internet than they did over the Internet. However, the gap between the percentage of non-financial sector businesses using the Internet and other ICT for selling has been closing. In 2005, 17 per cent of sales were made over non-Internet ICT, 8 per cent up on the 2004 figure. The proportion of businesses selling over the Internet was up by 22 per cent, to 15 per cent. However, some businesses have reported an overlap between EDI transactions using the Internet and using other ICT, and these may have an impact on the figures reported.

Repeating the pattern of business use of the Internet, businesses with a larger number of employees are more likely to use other ICT for sales than smaller businesses. In 2005 the value of sales over other ICT reached £88 billion for businesses employing 1,000 or more people and £59 billion for those employing between 250 and 999 (Figure 4.8). In 2005 sales over other ICT accounted for £66 in every £100 sold over all ICT (including the Internet) although this was a reduction from

# Figure **4.8**

### Value of sales over ICT¹ other than the Internet: by number of employees²

United Kingdom

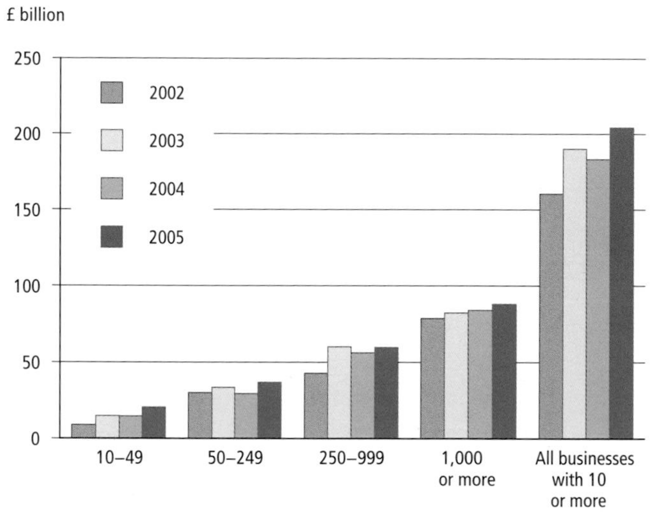

£ billion

1  Includes Electronic Data Interchange, email, computer-based fax and automated telephone entry.
2  Non-financial sector businesses.

*Source: e-Commerce Survey, Office for National Statistics*

the 2004 figure of £73 in every £100 and the 2003 figure of £83 in every £100 of sales over all ICT.

The manufacturing sector, with £109 billion of sales, followed by the wholesale, retail, catering and travel sector, with £74 billion worth of sales, together accounted for £90 of every £100 spent over other ICT in 2005. Post and telecommunication businesses were the most likely to buy over

other ICT. Interestingly, while similar proportions of businesses buy and sell over other ICT, as already reported, nearly four times more businesses buy than sell over the Internet.

## Business integration through ICT

ICT can generate performance improvements in business through integrating operations (see also Chapter 5: The wider economic impact of using ICT). Electronic links between business processes (e-business) are an aspect of this, and the ONS e-Commerce Survey attempts to identify business use of such links, specifically associated with e-buying and e-sellir g. These systems are usually linked to electronic systems for placing or receiving orders. Overall, 25 per cent of businesses with ten or more employees reported having an electronic system for placing or receiving orders (Table 4.9). The largest businesses with 1,000 or more employees were more than three times as likely as small businesses with between 10 and 49 employees to have such ICT systems for placing or receiving orders in 2005, at 72 per cent compared with 21 per cent.

With the low levels of e-integration of business processes reported, drawing conclusions at anything but the highest levels of aggregation is unwise. However, the pattern of use by size of business seen in the categories of linked electronic business processes is similar to that seen with all other types of ICT use. While electronic sales, purchases and use of websites offer some high profile measures of the impact of ICT, it is commonly recognised that the greatest potential for a positive impact is in productivity improvements through linking 'back room' systems electronically. In 2005, 8.7 per cent of businesses reported that their electronic ordering system linked

# Table **4.9**

### Businesses with electronic links between business systems: by number of employees

United Kingdom 2005

Percentages

|  | Number of employees | | | All businesses with 10 or more |
|---|---|---|---|---|
|  | 10–49 | 50–249 | 250–999 | 1,000 or more |  |
| Business with e-systems for placing or receiving orders | 21.2 | 37.5 | 55.1 | 71.7 | 24.8 |
| **Type of linked e-business systems** | | | | | |
| Production, service operations, logistics or delivery systems | 5.0 | 15.0 | 32.4 | 44.8 | 7.4 |
| Invoicing or payment systems | 5.9 | 17.4 | 36.8 | 57.0 | 8.7 |
| Suppliers' ordering or business systems | 6.2 | 11.1 | 22.0 | 42.1 | 7.6 |
| Customers' ordering or business systems | 4.1 | 11.0 | 23.4 | 31.7 | 5.8 |
| Internal system for re-ordering replacement supplies | 5.2 | 10.0 | 24.2 | 35.2 | 6.6 |

*Source: e-Commerce Survey, Office for National Statistics*

automatically with their invoicing or payment system. The larger the business the more likely it is to have ICT systems that automatically link with other ICT systems, either within the business or outside. This highlights the continuing pattern shown by the e-Commerce Survey that the largest businesses continue to lead the way in the take-up and exploitation of new technology.

When asked about e-links with other businesses, 7.6 per cent of businesses said that they had integrated external links with suppliers in 2005, and 5.8 per cent said they had external links with customers. Predictably, the larger the business, the more likely they were to have links to suppliers, with 22 per cent of businesses employing 250 to 999 people and 42 per cent of those employing 1,000 or more reporting these links.

## Access to the Internet at work

Almost nine out of ten businesses in the UK (89 per cent) reported access to the Internet by the end of 2005 (see also Chapter 8: Businesses and e-security).

The workplace is the second most common location after the home where people go online (see also Chapter 2: Accessing the Internet). In January to April 2006, 43 per cent of Internet users in employment in Great Britain went online at work. Rates of workplace Internet use varied by broad occupational category: 67 per cent of managers or professionals who were Internet users went online at work, compared with 45 per cent of users who worked in intermediate occupations and 26 per cent who worked in routine or manual occupations.

Of those who only went online in their workplace in the three months before interview in January to April 2006, 57 per cent sent emails, 64 per cent searched for information about goods and services, 59 per cent searched for information about travel and accommodation, 44 per cent surfed or browsed, and 31 per cent purchased online. There is a distinction between using the Internet at work and using it for work. According to research by the Oxford Internet Institute in 2003, 59 per cent of those who went online in their workplace in Great Britain said that it made them more productive to have the Internet at work, while 12 per cent said that it made them less productive.

The Internet is changing how people look for employment. In January to April 2006, 22 per cent of Internet users of working age in Great Britain had gone online to look for a job or to send in a job application in the three months before interview. Of these three-quarters (74 per cent) were in employment at the time they were interviewed.

## Computers and ICT use in agriculture in England

The Department for the Environment, Food and Rural Affairs (Defra) collected information on computer usage in England in its 2006 Farm Practices Survey. The survey focuses on farm business rather than personal use and does not include very small holdings.[3] Information on computer usage on agricultural holdings was previously collected by the December Survey of Agriculture. The two surveys are not directly comparable as the December survey covered all holdings, including the smallest ones, used a much larger sample size and a different analysis methodology.

In March 2006, 75 per cent of all holdings had access to a computer and most of these (75 per cent) had a computer on the farm and used it for farm business. Around one-fifth of holdings (19 per cent) that had a computer on the farm did not use it for farm business.

Among holdings that had a computer in 2006, 61 per cent had a computer that was less than three years old. For a further 25 per cent the computer on the holding was between three and six years old.

The main business use of computers on agricultural holdings was for financial or accounting purposes, carried out by 61 per cent of all holdings in 2006 (Figure 4.10). Over four in ten holdings (43 per cent) used the computer for operational

## Figure **4.10**

### Business use of computers on agricultural holdings: by reasons for use, 2006

England

Percentages

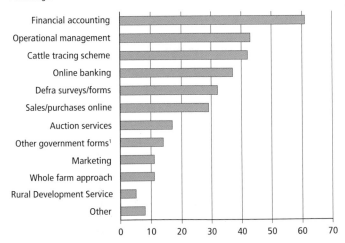

1 For example, tax credits.

*Source: 2006 Farm Practices Survey, Department for Environment, Food and Rural Affairs*

management, while 42 per cent used the cattle tracing system.[4] More than one-third (37 per cent) did online banking, while nearly one-third (32 per cent) used the computer for Defra forms and surveys.

Information was also gathered on the factors that would encourage use (or further use) of computers for farm business. The most common factor was improved computer skills, given by 57 per cent of those with no access to a computer and 46 per cent of those with access. This was followed by needing more time, given by 43 per cent and 48 per cent respectively. Confidence in computer security, for example viruses and confidentiality, was also a concern for 30 per cent of those with no access and 40 per cent of those with access to a computer.

## Notes and references

1   In this chapter when the size of the business is described in terms of number of employees, this includes all in employment in the business, including the owner.

2   Integrated Services Digital Network (ISDN). This is an international standard for switched, digital dial-up telephone service for voice and data. Analogue telephones and fax machines are used over ISDN lines, but their signals are converted into digital. Although developed in the early 1980s, it was more than a decade before ISDN became widely available. It enjoyed a surge of growth in the early days of the Internet, because it provided the only higher-speed alternative to analogue modems in many areas.

3   A holding is a production unit in the UK that is farmed or made available for farming. To be included in the Farm Practices Survey holdings must have at least 50 cattle, 100 sheep, 100 pigs or 1,000 poultry, or 20 hectares of arable crops or orchards.

4   The cattle tracing system website (CTS Online) allows farmers to:

- report cattle movements

- check the movement history of an individual animal

- record the death of an unregistered animal

- check the list of all cattle on the holding

- download information on cattle for use in the farm management programme

- register new calves online

- allow individual agent access to CTS Online

   More information can be found at www.defra.gov.uk/ANIMALH/ tracing/cattle/ctsonline.htm

## Introduction

Throughout the 1990s the rapid growth in both information and communication technology (ICT) investment and production was an important contributor to economic and productivity growth in the UK. In addition ICT investment has added to UK capital stock and capital services (which measure the contribution of capital stock to the production process). The investment in digital technology also affects the economy over the longer term by improving productive capacity and increasing efficiency.

### Computer hardware and software

Computer hardware is all the physical parts of a computer. It is capable of accepting and storing computer data, executing a systematic sequence of operations on computer data, and producing outputs, such as printouts.

Computer software provides instructions for the computer to perform each particular task. It tells the hardware how to process the data.

## ICT investment

As Chapter 4: e-Business highlights, a growing number of businesses have computers and network capabilities. The same is true across central and local government (see Chapter 7: e-Government). Many of the products bought, including software and telecommunication services, are recorded as investment since they provide a return over several years.

The analysis of ICT investment and production in this chapter is based on the *Blue Book*.[1,2] The data have been derived from the input-output annual supply and use tables that provide a time series from 1992. Recent work in the Office for National Statistics (ONS) to improve estimates of software investment by applying new methodology in line with international guidance has provided estimates of own-account software investment.[3] These estimates show a rise in total software investment as a proportion of gross domestic product (GDP) in 1999 from 0.8 per cent to 1.8 per cent. In 2003 total software investment was 1.9 per cent of GDP. Results from this study are being considered as part of the revisions process for the *Blue Book*.

Business investment in ICT products, both goods and services, more than doubled between 1992 and 2004, outpacing growth in total investment (Figure 5.1). Investment in ICT grew by 165 per cent between 1992 and 2000, and by 117 per cent between 1992 and 2004. Growth in total investment rose steadily over the same periods, from 68 per cent between 1992 and 2000 to 101 per cent between 1992 and 2004.

## Figure **5.1**

### Investment: ICT growth relative to the economy

**United Kingdom**

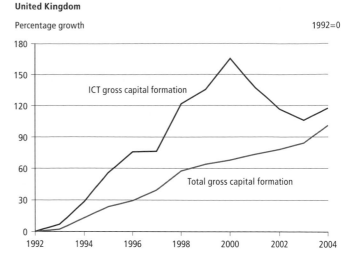

Source: United Kingdom Input-Output Analyses, Office for National Statistics

Although ICT investment levels were much higher in 2004 than in 1992, £28.6 billion compared with £13.1 billion, ICT investment had fallen from its peak of £34.9 billion in 2000 (Figure 5.2). This picture is mirrored in other parts of the world, such as the US. The decline in investment was most prominent in office machinery and computers, and other ICT. Software investment, which is included under telecoms and computer services, has flattened since 2000, dipping slightly in 2003 before rising in 2004.

## Figure **5.2**

### ICT investment: by product

**United Kingdom**

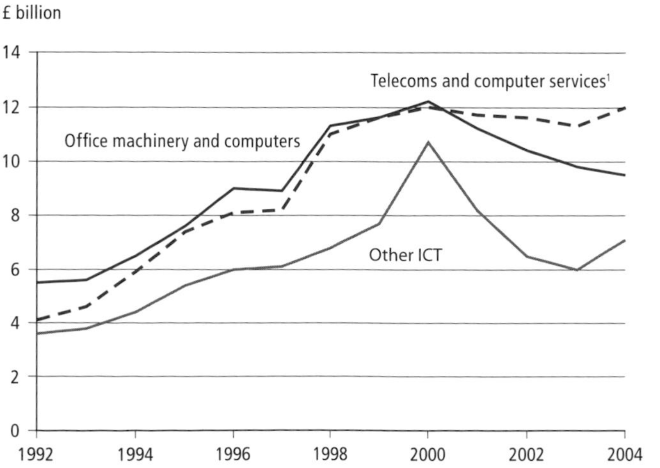

£ billion

1  Includes electronic instruments and software.

Source: United Kingdom Input-Output Analyses, Office for National Statistics

There are two main possible explanations for the high levels of investment in the run up to 2000 and the subsequent decline. First there was the 'dot-com' bubble in the late 1990s – a period when investing in Internet companies and technologies was particularly attractive. Internet companies, however, were soon deemed to be overvalued and the bubble burst. This, combined with a global slowdown in economic growth at the beginning of the century, delayed firms' decisions to invest. Companies were also afraid of the potential effects of the Millennium.[4] To protect against this companies invested heavily in hardware and software in the run up to the Millennium, possibly reducing the need for further investment in the subsequent years.

Although growth in ICT investment has been high, the ICT component of total investment is much smaller than the level of investment in other assets such as buildings, offices and other structures, and vehicles. In 2004 ICT investment was 14 per cent of total UK investment, compared with 13 per cent in 1992.

Like business investment, household consumption of ICT products has risen rapidly, more than doubling from £13.8 billion in 1992 to £31.2 billion in 2004. Much of this consumption is concentrated on products such as home computers, satellite dishes, digital television services, CD players, DVD equipment, digital cameras, MP3 players and mobile phones, see Chapter 1: Use of ICT among Households and Individuals.

While just less than one-quarter of the total supply of ICT goods and services is imported, computer imports exceed UK production. The UK was a net importer (imports less exports) of ICT products in each year between 1992 and 2004. In 2004 the trade deficit (the excess of imports over exports) in ICT products was £11.2 billion, the largest to date. The main products were computers and television-related equipment, where the UK imports components and assembles them into a final product for either export or domestic consumption, or imports goods directly for final consumption.

## Direct effect of ICT on the economy

ICT has contributed to economic growth in two ways: directly through the ICT producing industries, these include the software consultancies and computer manufacturers; and indirectly, through investments in ICT by the ICT consuming or using industries, for example, a clothing manufacturer investing in computers to aid design. This section considers the direct effect of ICT on the economy. The following section looks at some of the wider impacts of using ICT.

One way of examining the effect of the ICT sector on the economy is to look at how much added value it generates – that is, what is left after the intermediate purchases used in the production process are taken away from the total output of the ICT sector. For example, a computer manufacturer will have to purchase various components to build a computer. The computer is then sold at a higher price than the sum of all the individual components. The firm has added value – people value a built computer more than the individual components.

The ICT sector's gross value added (GVA) has increased every year since 1992. In 2004 the contribution of ICT to UK GVA accounted for £66.4 billion out of a total of £1,044.2 billion (6.4 per cent of the total). This growth was much faster than whole economy GVA growth over the last decade. From 1992 to 2004 GVA for the ICT sector grew by 125 per cent compared with whole economy GVA growth of 91 per cent (Figure 5.3).

## Figure 5.3

### Gross value added (GVA): ICT sector growth relative to the economy

**United Kingdom**

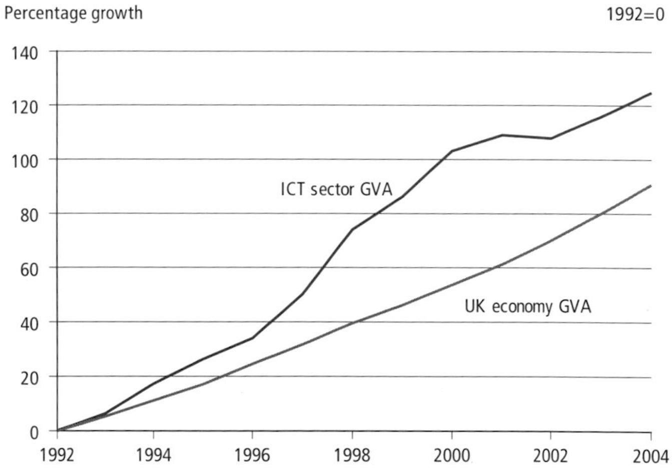

Percentage growth                                          1992=0

Source: United Kingdom Input-Output Analyses, Office for National Statistics

The growth in GVA generated by the ICT sector was led by the service industries rather than manufacturing industries (Figure 5.4). The services component grew by 164 per cent between 1992 and 2004, reaching £57.4 billion. Service industries are highly labour intensive, with compensation of employees (mainly wages and salaries, and the value of benefits from employers) accounting for nearly two-thirds of income generated by the ICT sector.

# Figure **5.4**

## ICT gross value added: manufacturing and services

**United Kingdom**

£ billion

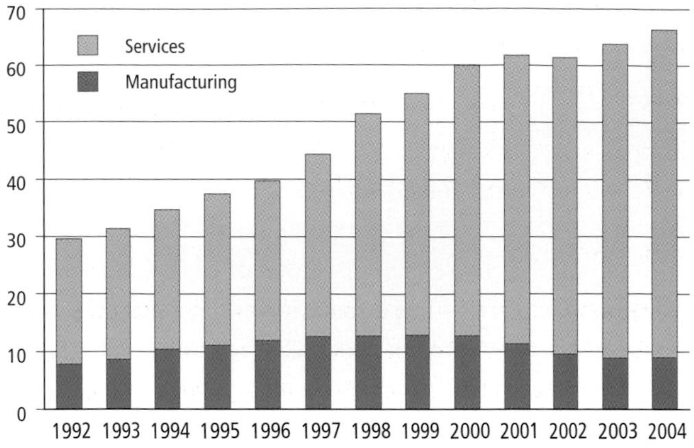

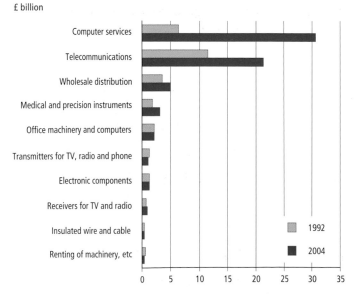

Source: United Kingdom Input-Output Analyses, Office for National Statistics

The strongest growth in GVA occurred in computer services, up from £6.4 billion to £30.6 billion, and in the telecommunications industries, from £11.5 billion to £21.3 billion (Figure 5.5). Manufacturing ICT GVA peaked at £12.7 billion in 1999, but has since fallen to £8.9 billion in 2004. Around one-third of this decline came from the office machinery industry group; its contribution to GVA peaked in 1998 and then fell in each of the subsequent years, from £3.3 billion in 1998 to £2.1 billion in 2004.

# Figure **5.5**

## ICT gross value added: by industry

**United Kingdom**

£ billion

Source: United Kingdom Input-Output Analyses, Office for National Statistics

Despite the relatively low contribution to ICT GVA from manufacturing, ICT has had a major impact on the sector. UK manufacturing output as a whole grew in current prices by 35 per cent between 1992 and 2004, more than the ICT manufacturing sector. However these figures are distorted by price changes. Prices of ICT products fell dramatically over this period. The price index for computers and other data processing equipment, for example, fell from 386 in 1992 to 47.5 in 2004 (where 2000=100). In contrast other manufacturing prices have generally risen over the period. If these price effects are removed, UK manufacturing growth in real terms during the 1990s was entirely a result of the rapid rise in ICT activity.

## Wider economic impact of using ICT

Through the 1990s there was considerable debate about the effects of information technology (IT) on economic performance in the US and other western economies. The paradox noted by US economist Robert Solow[5] that 'we see computers everywhere except in the productivity statistics' seemed to be supported by national data on investment and output.

In the period up to when the ICT bubble burst in 1999/2000, leading analysts disagreed as to whether the apparent improvement in productivity that accompanied the investment boom was just a result of cyclical effects, and would die away as the economy 'cooled off', or whether there was actually an underlying trend of higher productivity.

While the debate over the existence of a 'new economy' went on, central government departments, local government, businesses and households continued to buy ICT products. The focus of analysis started to move from the effect on national productivity brought about by the growth in the ICT producing industries to examining the benefits of ICT investment and use in other industries.

After 2000 research from the US showed that productivity in certain user sectors had continued to improve despite the pause in overall economic growth in 2001/02. Comparisons with Europe confirmed that US productivity growth was consistently positive in 'high ICT using' sectors such as wholesale and retail distribution, and financial services.[6] ICT contributed to growth in UK industries over recent years, but less fast than in the US.[7]

## Business behaviour and ICT

Gains that can be achieved by firms investing in and using ICT include:

- automating routine processes and substituting IT enabled machines for unskilled manual processes

- sharing information on customers and business processes within firms, which enables good practice to be shared more rapidly between employees

- better coordination and optimisation between operating processes within firms, to reduce waste and unused capacity

- improved tracking and modelling of demand patterns, permitting more efficient use of stocks

- faster links between firms, enabling 'just in time' approaches to delivery of materials and finished goods, reducing the need for stocks

- links, through the Internet or other communications networks, to suppliers and customers that can reduce the costs of transactions through automation, and also give access to wider markets

- better transfer of information between and within firms, and with sources of technical knowledge, which can make the processes of product and process innovation more efficient and effective

Firm-level analysis of productivity and ICT by ONS has looked at the behaviour of firms that invest in computer hardware and software, with employees who are IT enabled, which use electronic processes to buy, sell and coordinate operations, and that are heavy users of communications services.[8] This analysis has helped to shed light on how ICT has improved economic performance.

All studies of IT effects in business are affected by the problem of disentangling causality. Firms that invest in IT are usually those with the most skilled workers, the most innovative managers, larger scale operations, better international links, higher general investment levels, and located in the most prosperous areas.

Analysis of this firm-level data from ONS surveys confirms that:

- IT investment in manufacturing is strongly linked to investment in other assets, such as employee pay and skills

- Investment in hardware is strongly linked to firm size, with larger firms making larger investments

- US-owned firms invest more in hardware than similar UK firms, or than other multinational enterprises

- IT investment for firms in similar size bands and sectors shows significant regional variations, with higher investment in the South East and London, and lower investment in Scotland

These factors are taken into account in the analyses that follow. However, this area is one in which economists are still assembling a picture of rapid change.

### e-Commerce

ICT use in buying and selling (see Chapter 4: Buying and selling over the Internet, and Buying and selling over non-Internet ICT) makes many manufacturing markets more price sensitive.[9] Electronic procurement has made bidding processes more competitive, as well as extending the range of possible suppliers. Price effects show up in a number of industries. For example, mechanical engineering companies that used ICT had generally lower prices with the gap between e-sellers and non-e-sellers widening between 1997 and 2000 (Figure 5.6).

There are efficiency gains associated with e-selling. In many manufacturing sectors these are passed on to customers. Recent work using UK data shows that the price gap between e-sellers and non-e-sellers is levelling out, as stronger price competition spreads across markets. It also shows productivity gains are associated with e-commerce in service firms, especially in wholesaling, and for established retailers.

### Figure 5.6

**Prices in mechanical engineering: by whether companies are e-sellers or not**

United Kingdom

Relative price                                                    1995=100

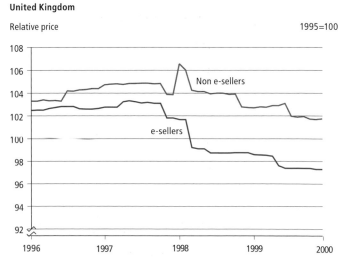

Source: e-Commerce and Firm Productivity, (Criscuolo and Waldron, Economic Trends No. 600), 2003

# Figure **5.7**

## Labour productivity and e-business in manufacturing

**United Kingdom**

Value added per employee (£000s)

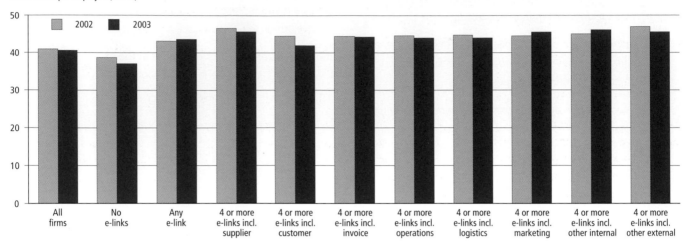

*Source: Annual Business Inquiry and e-Commerce Survey, Office for National Statistics*

## e-Business processes

The majority of electronic links within firms are not related to buying and selling, but to other operating processes such as production or service operating systems, delivery systems, invoicing or payment systems, marketing systems, suppliers' or customers' business systems. Since 2002 ONS surveys have measured some of these links, following similar work in the US. The UK results show that more networked and integrated processes led to high labour productivity levels.

Productivity in manufacturing firms in the UK with any e-link was higher than that of all firms, and was higher still for firms with four or more e-links (Figure 5.7). Productivity in firms with

no links was lower than that of all firms. For example, in 2003 value added per employee for manufacturing companies with at least four links, including integration with suppliers' systems was £45,700 compared with £37,100 for manufacturing companies without any links. A similar picture was found in the service sector, where value added per employee for companies with at least four links including customer relationship management systems was £45,500 in 2003 compared with £33,400 for companies with no links (Figure 5.8). Most productive service firms have multiple electronic links including customer business systems, suggesting that IT enables them to benefit from managing customer links more effectively.

# Figure **5.8**

## Labour productivity and e-business in services

**United Kingdom**

Value added per employee (£000s)

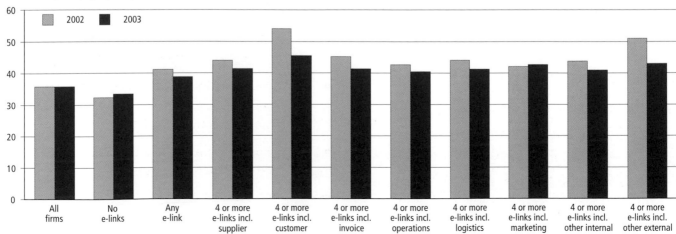

*Source: Annual Business Inquiry and e-Commerce Survey, Office for National Statistics*

## IT investment in hardware and software

Research published in 2005 by the London School of Economics (LSE) and ONS[10,11] on results for individual firms shows that investment in computer hardware and software by UK firms has, overall, improved output and productivity by more than its cost. Positive returns are shown for IT investment across manufacturing and service sectors, and in sectors that are high IT users as well as those that are less IT-intensive. This analysis does not include the effect of communications spending on productivity, which is covered later.

Two interesting features of this analysis may help to 'explain' the macroeconomic conclusion that IT returns have been lower in the UK than in the US. US firms are on average 3 per cent more productive than other multinationals, and 8 per cent more productive than UK domestic firms. Over 80 per cent of this productivity advantage is related to their investment in IT. Within IT intensive sectors, doubling of IT hardware is associated with 2 per cent higher productivity for UK domestic firms, 2.5 per cent for non-US multinationals, and 5 per cent for US multinationals. LSE research suggests this is because US firms use IT more efficiently and effectively.

In manufacturing, the productivity effects of hardware and software are 30 per cent greater in younger manufacturing firms than in older firms, which suggests productivity gains would be larger in economies, like that of the US, which have large numbers of new firms that grow successfully.

## ICT-equipped employees

ONS work using data from the e-commerce survey[12] linked to firm performance data shows that use of computers and the Internet by employees is strongly linked to higher productivity. This is after taking account of IT investment, which shows that there is a real and identifiable gain from firms engaging employees directly with IT. The measure (percentage employee use of computers or of Internet) shows strong productivity effects in manufacturing of 2.2 per cent for every additional 10 per cent of employees who are IT enabled, and 2.9 per cent for every additional 10 per cent of employees who are Internet enabled.

For younger manufacturing firms the effects are stronger still – 4.4 per cent for every additional 10 per cent of employees who are IT enabled, and 3.4 per cent for every additional 10 per cent of employees who are Internet enabled.

In service firms only younger firms show statistically significant productivity benefit linked to employees using Internet – 1.7 per cent for every additional 10 per cent of employees who are Internet enabled.

This difference is partly because of the international definition of computers used by employees in service sectors such as retailing. Organisation for Economic Co-operation and Development (OECD) and Eurostat surveys exclude electronic point of sale equipment – the technology that most retail employees use. In practice many electronic point of sale units include processing power similar to simple personal computers (PCs), so there may be measurement issues here. It suggests more work needs to be done in measuring IT use.

## Telecommunications spending

ONS studies have also looked at the separate effects of communications on productivity and the relationship to IT.[11] Across manufacturing and services there is a consistent, positive, productivity effect associated with telecoms service spending by firms.

In manufacturing firms the effects of communications spending are tied to hardware investment and employee use. Firms that make use of communications to link IT resources and employees achieve the greatest productivity gains.

In services, hardware capital, software capital, telecoms spend and the interaction between them all have significant effects. This suggests a wider and more varied range of IT effects on business productivity in services. The impact of telecoms use on productivity appears to be greatest in distribution services (wholesaling and retailing).

## Broadband

More recent work[13] by ONS and LSE has looked at the impact of broadband availability and use in businesses. This analysis showed that broadband users are more likely to have multiple business links and are more likely to automate new business processes. The effect on productivity shown in earlier work, where businesses with multiple links enjoy higher labour productivity is further compounded with the use of broadband technology.

The study concluded that:

- broadband adoption was related to e-commerce, ICT-equipped labour intensity and external demand

- investment in hardware is higher in regions and sectors with broadband availability especially for UK domestic firms in non-IT intensive industries

- early adopters of broadband experienced higher telecommunication costs but these declined over time

- broadband users are more likely to have multiple business links

- multiple links with broadband technology improve labour productivity

- firms with high broadband equipped labour share have higher productivity

## Notes and references

1   Mahajan S (2006) *United Kingdom Input-Output Analyses 2006 Edition*, www.statistics.gov.uk/statbase/Product.asp?vlnk=7640

2   Definition of the ICT manufacturing and services sector, from OECD (2002) *Measuring the Information Economy*. Organisation for Economic Co-operation and Development Paper:

**Manufacturing**

Office machinery and computers

Insulated wire and cable

Electronic valves and tubes and other electronic components

Television and radio transmitters and apparatus for line telephony and line telegraphy

Television and radio receivers, sound or video recording or reproducing apparatus and associated goods

Electronic instruments and appliances for measuring, checking, testing, navigating and other purposes, except industrial process control equipment

Electronic industrial process control equipment

**Services**

Wholesale of electrical household appliances and radio and television goods

Wholesale of computers, computer peripheral equipment and software

Wholesale of other office machinery and equipment

Telecommunications

Renting of office machinery and equipment, including computers

Computer and related activities

3   Chesson A and Chamberlin G (2006) 'Survey-based measures of software investment in the UK', *Economic Trends* No. 627, Office for National Statistics.

4   The Millennium Bug, also known as the year 2000 problem or the Y2K problem, was the risk that a large proportion of computers would go wrong at midnight on 31 December 1999. Many computer programs were written well before the year 2000, and years were programmed using only the last two digits (for example '86' for 1986). It was feared that when the century changed, the dates would roll back to 1900 instead of moving to 2000, which would have caused date comparisons to produce incorrect results affecting the financial and other sectors. It was also thought that embedded systems, making use of similar date logic, might fail affecting utilities and other crucial infrastructure. Companies, organisations and governments worldwide checked and upgraded their computer systems in the run-up to the Millennium. This had a significant impact on the computer industry before and after the year 2000.

5   Solow, R M (1987) 'We'd better watch out', *New York Times* book review (July 12).

6   Van Ark B, Inklaar R and McGuckin R H (2002) *Changing Gear. Productivity, ICT and Service Industries: Europe and the United States*, Research Memorandum GD-60 University of Groningen, Groningen Growth and Development Centre.

7   Oulton N (2002) 'ICT and productivity growth in the UK', *Oxford Review of Economic Policy,* 18, No. 3.

8   There are various surveys that have been linked to do analysis of firm-level data from ONS surveys: the Business Survey into capitalised items; Quarterly Capital Expenditure; and the Annual Business Inquiry.

9   Criscuolo C and Waldron K (2003) 'E-commerce and firm productivity', *Economic Trends* No. 600, pp 39–51.

10  Bloom N, Sadun R and Van Reenan J (2005) *ICT and productivity: Evidence from a panel of UK establishments,* Centre for Economic Performance Working Paper, London School of Economics.

11  Sadun R (2005) 'The role of IT in firm productivity; evidence from UK micro data', *Economic Trends* No. 625, pp 55–64.

12  Farooqui S (2005) 'Information and communication technology use and productivity', *Economic Trends* No. 625, pp 65–73.

13  Farooqui S and Sadun R (2006), *Broadband availability, use and impact on returns to ICT in UK firms,* Organisation for Economic Co-operation and Development (OECD) Paper, Directorate for Science, Technology and Industry (DSTI) Committee for Information, Computer and Communications Policy (ICCP) IIS(2006)9.

# ICT in the International Economy

**Christina Forrest and Mark Leaver**
Office for National Statistics

Chapter 6

## Introduction

Perhaps one of the most interesting aspects of the digital age is its global nature. Along with other countries, the UK has seen rapid growth in information and communication technology (ICT) and broadband use in both business and households. As the use and impact of ICT has grown new international markets have opened up, and businesses and consumers are taking advantage of the lower prices resulting from the increased online competition. Production processes are also being reviewed. Firms can move parts of their business to other countries to take advantage of lower costs – a phenomenon called offshoring.

Many countries are making a concerted effort to increase the level of adoption of, and investment in, ICT. In 2000 the EU launched a wide ranging set of reforms with the aim of the EU becoming 'the most dynamic and competitive knowledge-based economy in the world by 2010'. ICT initiatives have been set up as a result, first with the e-Europe 2005 action plan, which centred on encouraging broadband roll-out, followed by i2010, a five year strategy to boost the digital economy in the EU.

### Eurostat data

Data produced for Eurostat for e-commerce cover slightly different industries than results published by the Office for National Statistics (ONS) in the UK. Data for the UK quoted in this chapter are not on the same basis as those in Chapter 4: e-Business, and so are not directly comparable. They are, however, comparable with Eurostat data published for other countries.

Year dates used by Eurostat refer to the year in which the survey data were collected. In this chapter, Eurostat data items for the UK in relation to 2006 were derived from the 2005 UK e-commerce survey.

### International comparisons

There have been a number of international ICT benchmarking studies undertaken in recent years. In 2002 the UK Government commissioned a report comparing the UK e-economy with the other Group of Seven (G7) countries, plus Australia and Sweden.[1] The e-economy was defined as 'the dynamic system of interactions between a nation's citizens, business and government that capitalise upon online technology to achieve a social or economic good'. The report concluded that the UK, along with the US and Canada, had a relatively fertile market and political environments for e-commerce driven by the large skills base and availability of finance to support innovation. UK weaknesses, relative to the benchmarked set of countries, were in citizen and government uptake.

A similar study, which utilised several of the variables contained in the 2002 study but this time focusing on e-government, was released in November 2005. The report, *Beyond e-Government*,[2] concluded that e-government remains a priority for the countries studied, all of which have favourable market environments for delivering major ICT-enabled transformation. The focus of e-government was on ICT-enabled business transformation.

Policy in the EU is aimed at creating a 'knowledge economy', which is broader than an e-economy and incorporates research and development as well as the advance in ICT use and impact. As the name implies, skills form an integral part of the knowledge economy. Literacy is a prerequisite, but for such an economy to flourish advanced skills are needed to support these high-skilled sectors.

Mathematics and science graduate skills are vital for research and development in the ICT sector. The UK has a relatively high proportion of science and technology graduates, 18 per cent compared with 13 per cent in the EU and 10 per cent in the US in 2004 suggesting that it has a good supply of skilled workers entering the marketplace. In 2004 IT occupations made up just

### Figure **6.1**

### ICT-related occupations in the total economy in selected countries

Percentages

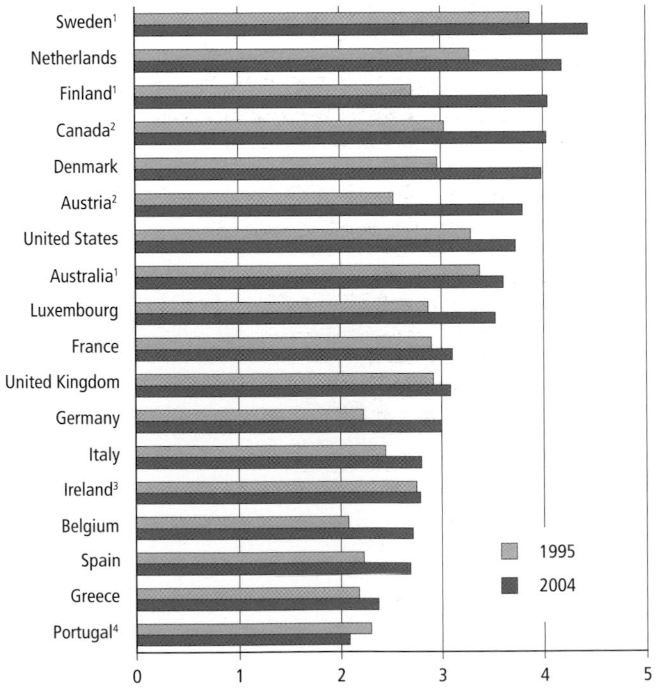

1  1997 instead of 1995.
2  2003 instead of 2004.
3  1999 instead of 1995.
4  1998 instead of 1995.

*Source: Organisation for Economic Co-operation and Development*

more than 3 per cent of total occupations in the UK, which was slightly more than the EU average (Figure 6.1). The Scandinavian countries and the US, all major ICT producers, were among the countries that had higher percentages of ICT-related occupations.

General users of ICT do not need such advanced skills but they need to have some level of computer literacy. Nearly all schools in the UK, and in other member states of the G7 and parts of Europe have computers and Internet access, although the number of computers per pupil varies.

ICT investment and research and development require finance. Financing methods vary across countries, which can make comparison difficult. For example, countries such as Germany and Japan traditionally have close relationships with banks whereas in the UK and the US the stock market has greater importance. One important source of finance for new firms is venture capital (capital that is invested in new or small high risk businesses). Between 2000 and 2003, 88 per cent of all venture capital investment in Ireland was in ICT, compared with 66 per cent in Canada and 62 per cent in the US. In the UK

22 per cent of all venture capital investment was in ICT, slightly less than the EU-15 average of 25 per cent.

The UK has one of the highest shares of IT expenditure relative to gross domestic product (GDP) – one of the main measures of economic activity – in Europe and is on a par with the US (Figure 6.2). Expenditure on IT hardware and software (see text box entitled Computer hardware and software on page 34 for definitions), IT equipment and other IT services in 2005 accounted for 4.2 per cent of GDP in the UK compared with 3.0 per cent of GDP across the EU as a whole.

Telecommunications expenditure is also relatively high in the UK compared with other countries, at 3.8 per cent of GDP in 2005, although the differences between countries are more modest (Figure 6.3). The largest shares of telecommunications expenditure in the EU are found in six of the ten states[3] that joined in May 2004, and in Portugal, reflecting a 'catch-up' with other European countries as businesses and households get connected to the Internet and invest in broadband. Telecommunications expenditure was 3.4 per cent of GDP in the EU-25 as a whole in 2005 compared with 7.4 per cent in

## Figure **6.2**

### IT expenditure as a percentage of GDP[1] in selected countries[2]

Percentages

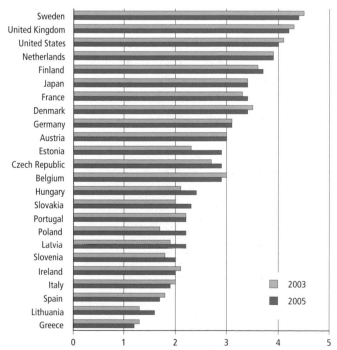

1 Annual data on expenditure for IT hardware, equipment, software and other services as a percentage of gross domestic product.
2 Eurostat data are not compiled on the same basis as data published by the ONS for the UK, see text box entitled Eurostat data at the beginning of this chapter.

*Source: Eurostat*

## Figure **6.3**

### Telecommunications expenditure as a percentage of GDP[1] in selected countries[2]

Percentages

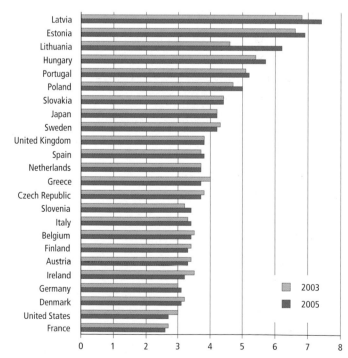

1 Annual data on expenditure for IT hardware, equipment, software and other services as a percentage of gross domestic product.
2 Eurostat data are not compiled on the same basis as data published by the ONS for the UK, see text box entitled Eurostat data at the beginning of this chapter.

*Source: Eurostat*

Latvia, 6.9 per cent in Estonia, 6.2 per cent in Lithuania, 5.7 per cent in Hungary, 5.2 per cent in Portugal and 5.0 per cent in Poland.

Much of ICT investment promotes innovation both in the ICT-producing sectors and in the ICT-using sectors. Innovations are vital to stay competitive in fast moving markets, hence the ICT sector invests heavily in research and development. These innovations are then translated into innovations in the IT-using sectors. In 2003 the highest research and development expenditure as a percentage of business enterprise sector research and development expenditure in the ICT sectors among member states of the Organisation for Economic Co-operation and Development (OECD)[4] occurred in Finland and Korea (Figure 6.4). Ireland had the largest proportion of research and development expenditure in ICT manufacturing and services combined, at 70 per cent, although data were for 2001. These shares reflect different developments in these countries. Ireland has attracted significant ICT inward investment. Finland is the home country of the world's leading mobile phone and fixed telecoms networks supplier and had the largest proportion on research and development

## Figure **6.4**

### Research and development expenditure[1] in ICT manufacturing and service industries in selected countries, 2003

Percentages

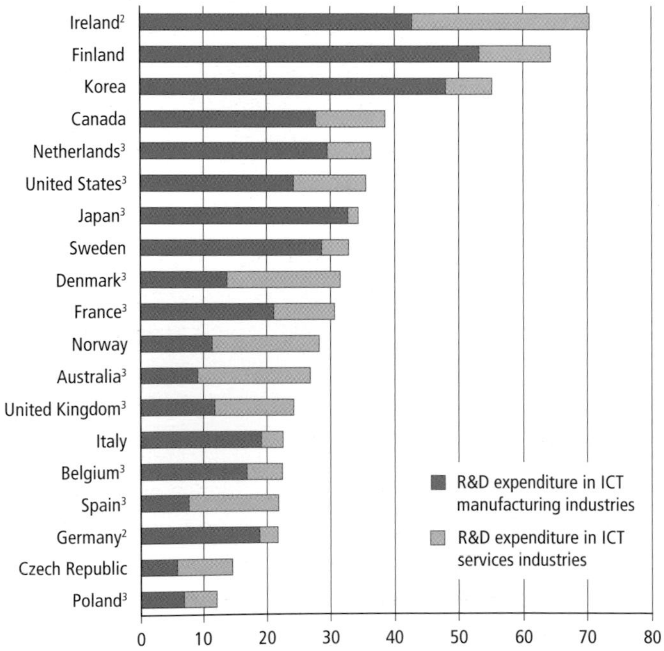

1  As a percentage of business enterprise sector research and development expenditure.
2  Data are for 2001.
3  Data are for 2002.

*Source: Organisation for Economic Co-operation and Development*

expenditure in ICT manufacturing industries. High research and development in ICT in Korea are a result of inward investment and broadband development. Research and development expenditure in all three countries was significantly higher in ICT manufacturing industries than in ICT services industries – 43 per cent compared with 28 per cent in Ireland, 53 per cent compared with 11 per cent in Finland and 48 per cent compared with 7 per cent in Korea. In the UK, research and development expenditure in ICT services industries was slightly higher than in ICT manufacturing industries, slightly more than 12 per cent compared with slightly less than 12 per cent.

A knowledge economy requires a fast network connecting businesses, citizens and government. Internet availability is almost everywhere in developed countries and broadband availability has been increasing rapidly. The more common broadband technology requires standard telephone lines to be upgraded and while most lines in European towns have been upgraded, some rural areas are relatively under served. Along with cable, digital subscriber lines (DSLs) are the most common ways of delivering broadband, see also Chapter 2: Connecting to the Internet. Among the OECD countries, Belgium, Korea, Luxembourg, The Netherlands and the UK all had 100 per cent DSL availability by mid-2005. The number of DSLs is increasing rapidly in other countries. Between 2004 and 2005 DSL availability in Ireland had increased from 74 per cent to 90 per cent of the country, in Hungary, from 65 per cent to 75 per cent, and in Slovakia, from 50 per cent to 60 per cent. Across the OECD availability was lowest in Greece, at 9 per cent.

As the supply of Internet and broadband services has increased, costs of connecting have fallen, driving fast growth in the number of business and citizens using them. Standard (non-broadband) Internet access has generally reached saturation among medium to large enterprises (50 or more employees) across the EU-25 member states. It is now broadband, rather than standard Internet access that has become the main policy priority across Europe. Broadband connection growth among businesses has been particularly strong in the UK and while it lagged behind the average of the other (then) 14 member states at the end of 2003, at 29 per cent compared with 40 per cent of enterprises with ten or more employees, it had caught up with the EU-25 average by 2006 (Figure 6.5). Between 2003 and 2006 the proportion of UK enterprises with ten or more employees having broadband connection increased by more than two-and-a-half-times, from 29 per cent to 77 per cent. Broadband use was highest in the Scandinavian countries, Spain, France, Belgium and The Netherlands, with between 82 per cent and 89 per cent of enterprises having broadband, and was approaching saturation among the largest enterprises. See also Chapter 4: ICT use in

## Figure **6.5**

### Enterprises[1] having a broadband connection,[2,3] 2006

**European Union–25**

Percentages

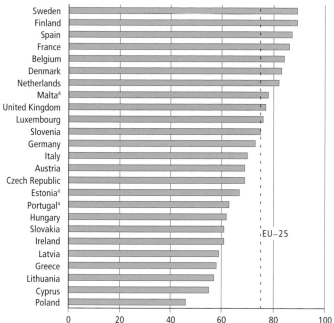

1  Enterprises with ten or more full-time employees.
2  The availability of broadband is measured by the percentage of
   enterprises that are connectable to an exchange that has been
   converted to support digital subscriber line (DSL) technology, to a
   cable network upgraded for Internet traffic, or to other broadband
   technology.
3  Eurostat data are not compiled on the same basis as data published
   by the ONS for the UK, see text box entitled Eurostat data at the
   beginning of this chapter.
4  Data for 2005.

*Source: Eurostat*

the UK, but note that data used there are collected on a
different basis so are not comparable with the Eurostat data
used here, see text box entilted Eurostat data at the beginning
of the chapter.

Many households do not have standard Internet access. The UK
compares favourably with other EU countries. Like them it has
continued to see a rise year on year. In 2006 the largest
proportions of households in Europe that had Internet access at
home were in the Scandinavian countries, particularly Iceland,
where 83 per cent of households were connected (Figure 6.6).
The next highest were The Netherlands, 80 per cent and
Denmark, 79 per cent. The UK, at 63 per cent, was above the
EU-25 average of 52 per cent of households. The ten states
that joined the EU in May 2004[3] generally had the lowest
proportions of household Internet access. Of these, Slovenia
had the highest proportion of households with access to the
Internet at home, at 54 per cent.

## Figure **6.6**

### Level of Internet access in households[1] in selected countries, 2006

Percentages

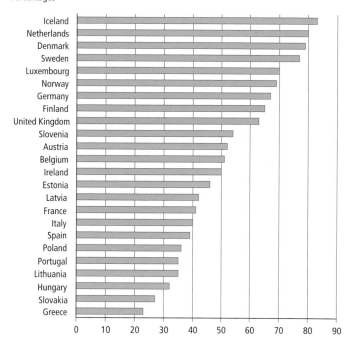

1  Eurostat data are not compiled on the same basis as data published
   by the ONS for the UK, see text box entitled Eurostat data at the
   beginning of this chapter.

*Source: Eurostat*

More and more households are connecting to broadband as
prices fall (see also Chapter 2: Connecting to the Internet).
Again the UK was above the EU-25 average, with the
proportion of households with a broadband connection as a
percentage of all households rising sharply from 16 per cent of
households in 2004 to 44 per cent in 2006 (Figure 6.7). The EU
average was around 32 per cent. Estonia had the highest level
of broadband connections among the ten states that joined the
EU in 2004, 37 per cent of households. There were large
differences in access to broadband across Europe and rates for
Greece (4 per cent), the Czech Republic (5 per cent), Slovakia
(11 per cent) Cyprus (12 per cent) and Ireland (13 per cent) were
especially low.

### e-Commerce

One of the major uses of the Internet is e-commerce – the
buying and selling of goods and services over electronic
networks – involving business to business as well as business to
customer and individual to individual transactions (see also
Chapter 4: ICT use). e-Commerce has opened up new
international markets for firms. A relatively small firm can now
export and import goods and services that previously may have
been logistically or financially unattractive. There are several
Internet portals and auction sites that bring together buyers

## Figure 6.7

### Households with a broadband connection[1] in selected countries,[2,3] 2006

Percentages

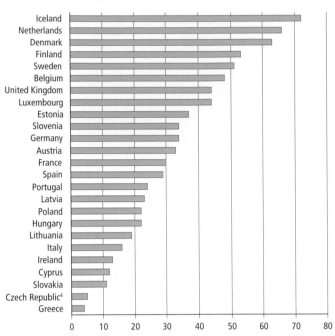

1  The availability of broadband is measured by the percentage of households that are connectable to an exchange that has been converted to support digital subscriber line (DSL) technology, to a cable network upgraded for Internet traffic, or to other broadband technologies.
2  Access to the Internet and broadband is changing rapidly. Surveys to capture the development of these services have been developed since 2000 (2003 for the ten countries that joined the EU in 2004) and are settling in. No data are available for Malta.
3  Eurostat data are not compiled on the same basis as data published by the ONS for the UK, see text box entitled Eurostat data at the beginning of this chapter.
4  Data are for 2005.

*Source: Eurostat*

## Figure 6.8

### Proportion of enterprises[1] having received orders over the Internet or through non-Internet ICT[2,3]

European Union–25[4]

Percentages

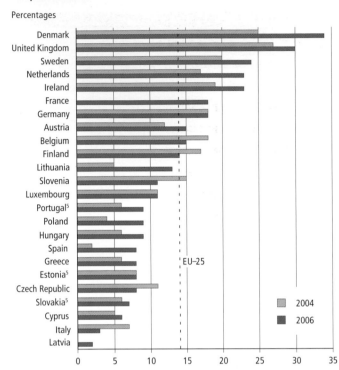

1  Enterprises with ten or more employees.
2  This indicator covers online selling through the Internet and Electronic Data Interchange (EDI) or other networks within the previous year. Only enterprises selling more than 1 per cent online are included.
3  Eurostat data are not compiled on the same basis as data published by the ONS for the UK, see text box entitled Eurostat data at the beginning of this chapter.
4  No data for Malta.
5  Data are for 2005.

*Source: Eurostat*

and sellers of goods and services on an international scale. e-Sellers can take advantage of increased demand particularly when domestic demand might be temporarily weak. e-Buyers can benefit from lower prices as a result of the increased competition.

e-Commerce use has increased among businesses and individuals across the EU. In 2006 the UK had the second highest percentage of enterprises receiving orders over the Internet or through non-Internet ICT in the EU, at 30 per cent, following Denmark, at 34 per cent (Figure 6.8). The EU-25 average was 14 per cent. Denmark showed the greatest proportional increase between 2004 and 2006, from 25 per cent to 34 per cent, followed by Lithuania, which increased by 8 percentage points from 5 per cent to 13 per cent.

The UK also had one of the highest percentages in Europe of sales over the Internet as a proportion of total turnover, 6 per cent in 2006, four times the proportion in 2003 (Figure 6.9).

The volume in 2006, however, was dwarfed by that of Ireland, which had sales accounting for almost 10 per cent of total turnover. One reason for this could be that Ireland is one of the world's largest ICT exporters and in particular one of the largest software exporters. Internet sales are particularly attractive for digitised products such as software, which can simply be downloaded by the customer.

Retail and tourism are two sectors where business to customer e-commerce is booming according to the European Commission's *European e-Business Report*.[5] Tourism has seen a rise in large intermediaries offering customers a wide range of airlines, hotels and tour operators. But while a large proportion of transactions are made online in this sector, the report notes that for other products customers also use the Internet to search for information and then buy the product in a shop, see Chapter 2: e-shopping.

## Figure **6.9**

### Percentage of total turnover[1] from e-commerce over the internet[2] in selected countries[3,4]

Percentages

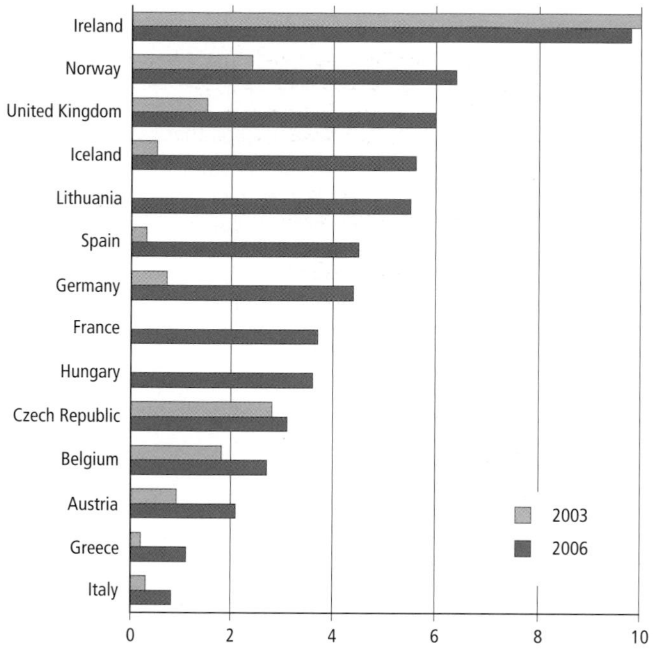

1 Enterprises with ten or more employees.
2 Information comes from the surveys carried out by the national statistical institutes on usage of ICT by enterprises. The indicator is calculated as the enterprises' receipts from sales through the Internet as percentage of the total turnover. Sales through other networks are not included, leaving out for instance Electronic Data Interchange-based sales.
3 Data for other EU members were either not available, uncertain or unreliable, and so have not been included.
4 Eurostat data are not compiled on the same basis as data published by the ONS for the UK, see text box entitled Eurostat data at the beginning of this chapter.

*Source: Eurostat*

## The global impact of ICT

The growth in ICT has accelerated globalisation (the increased international linkages and interdependency between countries). Globalisation can be seen in the growth in international trade and foreign direct investment as well as in the development of ICT such as the Internet, which have revolutionised the way individuals and business interact with each other.

International trade has risen rapidly over the last few years, and trade in ICT products has risen even faster, despite falls at the beginning of the century caused by the worldwide slump in economic growth and large falls in ICT investment. Since 2003 there has been a worldwide recovery led largely by the US and the phenomenal growth in Asian countries such as China.

Countries are becoming more specialised in ICT goods and services production. In terms of absolute value, the US and Ireland are the largest OECD exporters of ICT goods and services respectively. According to the OECD, in 2004 Ireland

exported $18.6 billion of computer and information services, the UK exported $10.5 billion and the US $8.5 billion. Despite being the largest exporter of ICT goods, the US had a trade deficit in them (that is it imports more than it exports) and unlike Ireland, ICT goods exports formed a relatively small part of its economy as measured by GDP.

International trade cannot be analysed in isolation from foreign direct investment, particularly in the ICT sector since much trade is conducted by multinational enterprises. In Ireland, for instance, many of the large ICT exporters are US-owned firms operating there to serve Europe. Inward foreign direct investment flows into the UK peaked in 2000, but then fell dramatically as a result of the large fall in mergers and acquisitions that accompanied the global slowdown.

Research has shown that US multinationals in the UK are more productive than UK or other foreign-owned multinationals (see also Chapter 5: The wider impact of using ICT). The reasons for this are especially important for policy makers wishing to emulate the US productivity growth 'miracle' that has occurred in the last decade, especially in the sectors that are intensive users of ICT. Researchers from the London School of Economics have studied US multinationals in the UK to try and explain the US productivity differential.[6] Previously it has not been possible to distinguish if the gains arose from a superior environment in the US or if the gains actually stemmed from the internal organisation of US firms. By looking at US multinationals in the UK (that is outside the US environment) the researchers could directly identify if the gain came from the US organisation.

They found that US firms had much higher productivity resulting from their IT capital compared with other firms, be they other multinationals or purely domestic firms, and that this accounts for all the productivity difference between US firms and UK firms in the sectors in the sample that used ICT extensively. There are several possible reasons for this. Much emphasis is placed on the complementary investments that are needed for IT investments, such as changes in the organisational structure of the firm. A more devolved, highly skilled organisation, for example, may help the firm maximise the benefits of IT. Another reason may be that US firms are closer to the IT developers (many are in the US), which may give them an early advantage. Or, it could be that greater competition in the US because of less regulation has forced US firms to adapt quickly to new technology.

The advance in ICT combined with the growth in international trade and foreign direct investment has allowed firms not only to sell but also to move production abroad. Offshoring, the transferring of production to a foreign affiliate or a foreign external firm, has occurred for decades in goods production.

Manufacturing processes that do not require a high-skilled workforce have traditionally been offshored to countries with a large and relatively low-cost labour supply. Standard economic theory states that such specialisation should result in a net gain as countries concentrate on production where they have a relative efficiency. The firm gains from cheaper production, which may feed through into lower prices for the consumer.

Recent years have seen the emergence of the offshoring of services, which has attracted a lot of media interest. Because of the nature of the work, service sector firms have traditionally needed to be close to the customer but the advance of ICT, particularly telecommunications, has changed this. Call centres, for instance, can now be located abroad. As a general picture, services have traditionally been the preserve of developed countries. As countries have become more developed, agriculture and then manufacturing decline, while the share of service firms in the economy increases. This is a very rough picture but it is certainly evident in the UK, where services in 2005 represented around three-quarters of the economy. The possibility of UK offshoring processes abroad has been seen by parts of the media as a threat to UK jobs and to the economy as a whole.

It is difficult to measure the impact of offshoring accurately. There are no official UK data explicitly on offshoring, but it has been possible to look at imports of services and measure the effect they have had on the economy. High-skilled as well as low-skilled services are imported. In 2003 India was the fifth largest supplier to the UK computer services industry. India can supply a highly skilled, English-speaking but relatively cheap workforce, so it is a main contender for predominantly English-speaking firms.

As a whole, offshoring of services still appears to be quite low as measured by imports of knowledge-based business services as a proportion of GDP (1.2 per cent in 2001), primarily because it is such a new phenomenon. There is uncertainty involved that may make a firm wait a while before offshoring. For example, although production may be cheaper it needs to be determined whether it is of the same quality or as efficient as in the domestic country. Production may be ten times cheaper abroad but if it is ten times less productive there are actually no cost savings unless that productivity can be increased. A firm may be anxious about the loss of control or data confidentiality, which is particularly important in services where large volumes of data on customers are held. Indeed an EU firm may be restricted legally since it can only offshore to countries that have an equivalent of the *Data Protection Act* in force.

In general estimates of the impact of offshoring on the UK economy have shown little or no negative effect. IT and call centre occupations, two occupations that are considered to be susceptible to offshoring, have experienced strong employment growth in the UK and redundancy levels in these occupations have been falling in recent years.[7] One reason is that the UK is actually a net exporter of IT-enabled services, particularly businesses services where it has a large trade surplus. Private sector estimates of job losses as a direct result of offshoring are generally small and are often lower than the level of job losses that result from the natural turnover of jobs that occurs in any economy.

The productivity effects of offshoring of services are difficult to identify. The University of Nottingham, using data from Ireland, found that the offshoring of goods had a positive impact on productivity for firms that were part of international production networks (that is multinational end exporting firms) but that there was no such productivity gain associated with the offshoring of services, perhaps because the data only went up to 1998.[8] However, there are real business reasons why this might be the case. The paper reports one private sector survey finding that 56 per cent of respondents claim outsourced IT work was at least worse than that produced in-house.

ONS carried out a similar analysis for the UK in 2005.[9] This study found that firms that offshore services are mainly firms with international links because they are already either exporters of services or multinationals. Firms that offshore are on average larger, more capital intensive, use more ICT capital and pay higher wages than firms that do not offshore. The results identified some productivity gain from services offshoring for services sector firms, but that the effect is not statistically significant among manufacturing firms. The productivity effect comes mainly from firms that are domestic and non-globally engaged, that is they do not export and are not part of a multinational firm. This suggests that for firms already globally engaged the boost from offshoring has less of an impact than for firms for which it was their only international activity. Other research[10] has found that firms that are more ICT intensive purchase a greater amount of services on the market and that they are more likely to purchase offshore than less ICT intensive firms.

## Notes and references

1    Office for National Statistics *International e-Commerce Benchmarking Experimental Statistics* online report: www.statistics.gov.uk/StatBase/Product.asp?vlnk=9565

2    Booz, Allen and Hamilton (2005) *Beyond e-Government: The world's most successful technology-enabled transformations.* INSEAD, Paris. The full report, can be found at www.egov2005conference.gov.uk

3   The ten states that joined the EU in May 2004 were: Cyprus, the Czech Republic, Estonia, Hungary, Latvia, Lithuania, Malta, Poland, Slovakia and Slovenia.

4   The Organisation for Economic Co-operation and Development (OECD) is a forum where the governments of 30 market democracies work together to address the economic, social and governance challenges of globalisation as well as to exploit its opportunities.

5   e-Business Watch (2004) *The European e-Business Report 2004*. www.ebusiness-watch.org/resources/documents/eBusiness-Report-2004.pdf

6   Bloom N, Sadun R and van Reenen J (2005) *ICT and productivity: Evidence from a panel of UK establishments*, Centre for Economic Performance Working Paper, London School of Economics.

7   Heckley G (2005) Offshoring and the labour market, *Labour Market Trends* 113(9), pp 373–385, September 2005.

8   Gorg H, Hanley A and Strobl E (2005), *Productivity effects of international outsourcing: evidence from plant level data*, OECD Workshop on Globalisation November 2005.

9   Criscuolo C and Leaver M (2005), *Offshore outsourcing and productivity*, OECD Workshop on Globalisation November 2005.

10  Abromovsky L and Griffith R (2006), *Outsourcing and offshoring of business services: how important is IT?* AIM Research Working Paper www.aimresearch.org/workingpapers/029rgpaper.pdf

# e-Government

**Ewen McKinnon**
Cabinet Office
**Sarah Armitage**
NHS Direct
**Mark Pollard**
Office for National Statistics

Chapter 7

## Introduction

Information and communication technology (ICT) has the potential to transform the way that citizens and businesses interact with local and central government and this is recognised by *Transformational Government – enabled by technology*, a report published by the Cabinet Office in November 2005. The report notes that services delivered through electronic communication channels allow customers the opportunity to access public services at times and in ways that suit them. Public service providers in turn benefit from efficiencies as self-service channels[1] are taken up in greater numbers and resources are moved to the front line. And for both citizens and businesses ICT increases opportunities for being 'listened to' by government, supporting improved participation in democratic institutions.

## Background

The Prime Minister launched the 'UK online' campaign in September 2000 to get people and business online.[2] e-Government was also a key element of this campaign, with early activity focused on the modernisation of services by making the best use of new e-channels such as the Internet, interactive digital television, mobile phones and kiosks, and bespoke systems such as Electronic Data Interchange (EDI). By 2004, three-quarters of the services had been e-enabled and the UK ranked fifth out of the EU-25 for availability of 20 common European services, and third for the sophistication of the services made available online.[3]

Early progress on making e-services available was followed with policies and actions to increase usage. Usage targets were set for key e-services and service designers began to focus on user needs. This led to the development of one-stop-shops for online government services, such as www.direct.gov.uk for citizens and www.businesslink.gov.uk for businesses. These sites bring services and customers together in one place and promote cross-sell between services, driving take-up higher than would otherwise be achieved by delivering services through many individual departmental channels.

In 2005 policy in the UK shifted away from e-government as a specialised, separately identifiable policy area of service delivery to the broader modernisation policy using ICT to support the transformation of public services around the needs of citizens, businesses and frontline service providers. The Transformational Government strategy[4] focuses on customer-centric service delivery, shared services and professionalism as the foundations of a long-term programme of transformational change through ICT.

This chapter focuses on the situation in 2005 (the latest date that data are available) before the policy shift towards transformation government. Survey-based measurements of the use and impact of e-government channels at a national level are presented. Survey data are supplemented by operational data for specific services where available.

## Citizen-facing e-government

Before looking at who is using e-government it is worth assessing the level of general use of government services by any means of contact and then at the willingness of the population to switch to e-channels for their dealings with government. In the year to July 2005,[5] 82 per cent of the adult population in Great Britain contacted government, either local or central, on at least one occasion in the 12 months before interview. The most popular reason was health; 65 per cent contacted government on health matters, followed by contacts regarding tax, pensions and benefits, at 40 per cent (Figure 7.1). Contact with local government was lower, at 24 per cent.

### Figure **7.1**

**Individual contact[1] with government: by service area, 2004/05[2]**

**Great Britain**

Percentages

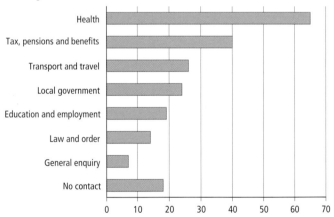

1   Adults aged 16 and over. In the 12 months before interview.
2   Data were collected in October 2004 and February, May and July 2005.
*Source: Omnibus Survey, Office for National Statistics*

While overall annual contact with government is generally high, it is also infrequent. Over three-quarters of the population had contacted government less than once a month, including nearly one-fifth (18 per cent) who had contacted government less than once a year.

The most popular methods for contacting government were the traditional ones of telephone (preferred by 86 per cent of adults), in-person visits (56 per cent) or post (55 per cent)

(Figure 7.2). In 2005, 44 per cent of adults were willing to use e-channels; a further 6 per cent who stated that they were not willing to use e-channels had contacted government using the Internet in the previous 12 months. The willingness to use e-channels was linked to age – older people were less inclined to use the new technology than younger people.

## Figure 7.2

### Individual preferences[1] for ways of contacting government, 2004/05[2]

**Great Britain**

Percentages

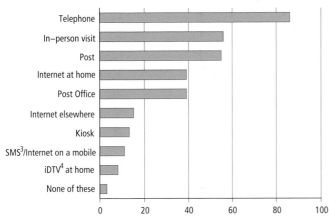

1  Adults aged 16 and over.
2  Data were collected in October 2004 and February, May and July 2005.
3  Short Messaging Service (or texting).
4  Interactive digital television.

*Source: Omnibus Survey, Office for National Statistics*

## Figure 7.3

### Reasons why Internet users[1] did not use government websites,[2] 2004/05[3]

**Great Britain**

Percentages

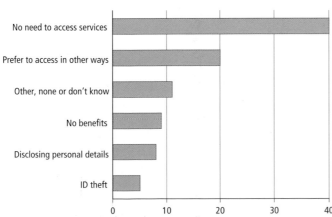

1  Adults aged 16 and over.
2  In the 12 months before interview.
3  Data were collected in October 2004 and February, May and July 2005.

*Source: Omnibus Survey, Office for National Statistics*

The main reason why adult Internet users did not access government websites was the lack of need to access these services, given by 40 per cent of those Internet users who did not use e-government services (Figure 7.3). This is similar to the main reason why adults did not access the Internet in the first place – non-users did not see a need to access the Internet, did not want to or had no interest in doing so,[6] see also Chapter 2: Profile of non-users of the Internet. Of those non-users who stated they had no need to access services, around three-quarters had contacted government in the last 12 months. In addition, two-fifths of non-users of government websites indicated that they would be willing to contact government through the Internet. These results suggest that there is clear potential for growth in e-government usage.

Internet users who do not use government websites were asked what would encourage them to do so. Tangible benefits such as time savings, reduced cost and faster response appeared to be the most popular potential triggers, given by 31 per cent, 30 per cent and 27 per cent respectively (Figure 7.4). For one-quarter of Internet users who did not use government, none of the potential benefits offered would encourage them to start doing so.

## Figure 7.4

### Triggers for Internet users[1] to use government websites, 2004/05[2]

**Great Britain**

Percentages

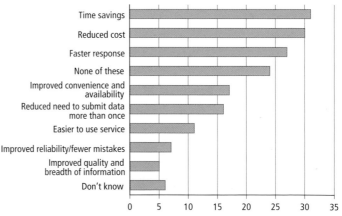

1  Adults aged 16 and over and who did not use government websites in the 12 months before interview.
2  Data were collected in October 2004 and February, May and July 2005.

*Source: Omnibus Survey, Office for National Statistics*

### Take-up of e-services

In July 2005, 58 per cent of Internet users had visited a government website in the previous 12 months before interview (Figure 7.5). Over this period the proportion of people

# Figure **7.5**

**Internet users[1] who have visited a government website**

Great Britain

Percentages

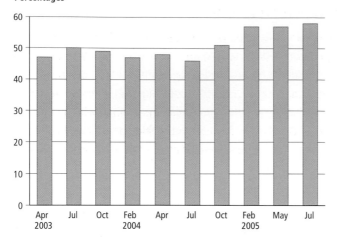

1  Adults aged 16 and over. In the 12 months before interview.

*Source: Omnibus Survey, Office for National Statistics*

# Table **7.6**

**Visitors to government websites:[1] by region**

Great Britain, 2004/05[2]                          Percentages

|  | Current Internet users[3] | Government website visitors |
|---|---|---|
| **England** | 60 | 56 |
| North East | 48 | 61 |
| North West | 59 | 55 |
| Yorkshire and The Humber | 54 | 48 |
| East Midlands | 62 | 55 |
| West Midlands | 54 | 52 |
| East | 66 | 56 |
| London | 65 | 60 |
| South East | 66 | 61 |
| South West | 61 | 57 |
| **Wales** | 54 | 43 |
| **Scotland** | 59 | 49 |

1  Visited websites in the 12 months before interview.
2  Data were collected in October 2004 and February, May and July 2005.
3  Adults aged 16 and over who have used the Internet in the three months before interview.

*Source: Omnibus Survey, Office for National Statistics*

using government websites increased by 12 percentage points. This increase coincides with the emergence of sites such as www.direct.gov.uk, launched in May 2004, which provide one-stop-shops for online government services and have rapidly grown to be among the most popular e-government sites.

An analysis of the demographics of government website usage, relative to the online adult population, indicates that Internet users who visited government websites were more likely than those who did not visit government websites to be economically active and of working age. Apart from the 16 to 24 age group, usage declined with age, with people in the 25 to 44 age group the most likely of all age groups to visit government websites. In general, regions that have large proportions of regular Internet users also have high proportions of users of government websites (Table 7.6). The exception was the North East, where there was a higher proportion of people who visited government websites compared with those who used the Internet regularly.[7] The North East and the South East have the highest proportions of people accessing government websites, at 61 per cent each.

Online e-government use was low for those at risk of social exclusion, particularly working-age people without qualifications, those in social housing and the elderly. One exception is that e-government use by those without work was found to be higher than average, reflecting the popularity of electronic job searches and www.jobcentreplus.gov.uk. Job seekers also use Job Centre kiosks for employment searches in addition to the Internet.

There is, as would be expected, a strong link between willingness to use the Internet to contact government and actual use of government websites. There does not appear to be a statistical association between willingness to use e-channels to deal with government and general contact frequency with government. These results therefore do not support the theory that those who are the most frequent users of government services are also the least likely to use the new electronic service delivery channels.

The most popular activity on government websites was gathering information, done by 28 per cent of adults in the 12 months before interview in the year to July 2005 (Table 7.7). The uptake of online e-government activities reduced with sophistication in a similar way to other web-based activities; 8 per cent downloaded forms, 6 per cent submitted an application form online and 3 per cent made a payment online. Availability of services also influences these results. There are clearly more informational government services available electronically than booking and payments services. Activity in these areas is likely to increase significantly with mass-market services such as 'Choose and Book' for hospital appointment bookings.

There is a gap between what people are willing to do on the Internet and what they are actually doing. For example, nearly

## Table **7.7**

### Activities on government websites, 2004/05[1]

Great Britain — Percentages

| | Adults who are willing to use government websites | Adults who use government websites[2] |
|---|---|---|
| Obtain information | 40 | 28 |
| Download form | 35 | 8 |
| Submit an application | 33 | 6 |
| Send email | 38 | 4 |
| Make a payment | 26 | 3 |
| Book an appointment | 33 | 1 |

1 Data were collected in October 2004 and February, May and July 2005.
2 Adults aged 16 and over. In the 12 months before interview.

Source: Omnibus Survey, Office for National Statistics

three-quarters of transactional government website visitors (that is people who visit a government website to request or receive a service) who haven't made a payment to government online, have shopped online. This suggests that people are capable of adopting more sophisticated online activities with government than they currently undertake.

Government services can also be accessed through non-Internet based e-channels such as automated telephony, kiosks, interactive digital television or Short Messaging Service (SMS or texting). In the 12 months to July 2005, 13 per cent of the adult population used government services through these channels and nearly half of these, 6 per cent, had not used Internet-based government services.

Only a few truly mass-market e-government services have been delivered in the UK. New large-scale services such as the ability to pay car tax electronically, which was launched in October 2006, are only now becoming available. As a result the population level analysis focused on so far masks progress within individual services. Table 7.8 presents annual operational

## Table **7.8**

### Take-up for selected e-government services,[1] 2005[2]

Great Britain — Percentages

| | |
|---|---|
| University applications | 73 |
| Driving test bookings (theory tests) | 51 |
| Land Registry Direct | 19 |
| Tax self-assessment forms | 17 |
| Pension forecasts | 11 |

1 By adults aged 16 and over.
2 Latest annual data available in autumn 2005.

Source: Autumn 2005 Performance Report, Cabinet Office

data available in autumn 2005 gathered by service delivery departments for specific services. e-Channel take-up is presented as a percentage of total transactions. The data suggest that the electronic take-up of some services is much higher than the population level data presented in Table 7.7.

### e-Government impact

People who use e-government services were asked about their experiences – both positive and negative. In the 12 months to July 2005 nine in ten users could identify at least one positive benefit that they had experienced, with greater convenience and availability being the most common, along with time savings. Over two in five users also claimed that they had experienced either cost savings associated with e-channels or increased responsiveness.

Around one-half of e-government users did have at least one negative experience. The most common complaint concerned usability of services and technical problems. The difficulty in finding services online was also an issue for 15 per cent of users, as were security problems.

Satisfaction and loyalty among e-government users were generally high. In the 12 months to July 2005, 90 per cent of users rated services as generally good, and 91 per cent indicated they would continue to use e-services in the future.

### NHS Direct Online

NHS Direct Online (www.nhsdirect.nhs.uk) is the main NHS health advice and information website for patients and the public.[8] It is one of a range of services provided by NHS Direct, which include a 24-hour confidential telephone helpline and an interactive service on digital satellite television

NHS Direct Online provides patients and the public with:

- an interactive self-help guide to treating common health problems at home

- an encyclopaedia covering hundreds of illnesses and conditions with links to other accredited third-party websites

- 'frequently asked questions' based on data from both the NHS Direct telephone service and the website's own online enquiry service about what the public is asking about

- details of local health services such as GPs, dentists and pharmacists

- news and features on current health issues an online

- enquiry service for requesting health information and

- interactive health quizzes

Since NHS Direct Online was launched in December 1999, usage has increased year on year (Figure 7.9). In 2001/02 the total number of visits to the website was just over 2 million, by 2004/05 this had risen to over 9 million visits. Usage of NHS Direct Online is generally highest during January, February and March.

The user profile of the website's health information enquiry service has remained largely the same over the three years since it was launched in 2002 (Table 7.10). In 2004/05 nearly two-thirds of enquiries (64 per cent) concerned female patients and a similar proportion (63 per cent) concerned people aged under 35. The most popular topics of enquiry were women's health and medicines, both at 7 per cent. The most visited areas of the NHS Direct Online website are its comprehensive health encyclopaedia and interactive self-help guide. Figures 7.11 and 7.12 show the top ten most frequently accessed topics within these during 2004/05.

## Figure **7.9**

### Number of NHS Direct Online visits

United Kingdom

Thousands

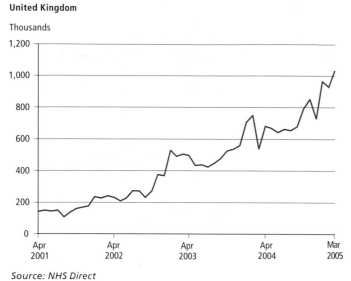

Source: NHS Direct

## Table **7.10**

### Usage of NHS Direct Online health information enquiry service: by sex and age

United Kingdom                                          Percentages

|  | 2002/03 | 2003/04 | 2004/05 |
|---|---|---|---|
| Male | 39 | 36 | 36 |
| Female | 61 | 64 | 64 |
| | | | |
| Age-groups | | | |
| 0–15 | 10 | 10 | 10 |
| 16–24 | 24 | 24 | 24 |
| 25–34 | 28 | 28 | 29 |
| 35–44 | 15 | 16 | 16 |
| 45–54 | 9 | 10 | 9 |
| 55–64 | 4 | 6 | 6 |
| 65 and over | 4 | 5 | 4 |
| Age not specified | 6 | 1 | 2 |
| | | | |
| All enquiries = 100% | 31, 346 | 47,325 | 42,958 |

Source: NHS Direct

## Figure **7.11**

### Most accessed topics in NHS Direct Online self-help guide, 2004/05

Number of visits, thousands

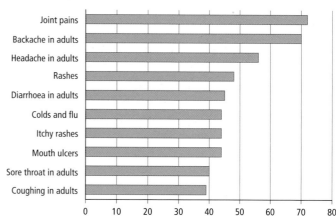

Source: NHS Direct

## Figure **7.12**

### Most accessed topics in NHS Direct Online health encyclopaedia, 2004/05

Number of visits, thousands

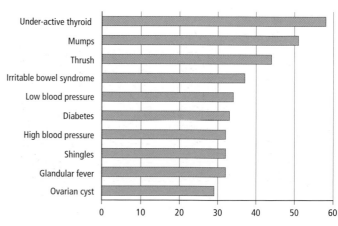

Source: NHS Direct

## Business-facing e-government

Around one-half of businesses with ten or more employees,[9] 51 per cent, reported electronic dealings with government departments and other public bodies during 2005, the most recent year for which data are held. This proportion has increased steadily since 2002, when 31 per cent of businesses with ten or more employees reported electronic interactions with public administrations. These interactions vary by both size of business and business activity.

The larger the business, the more likely it is to have electronic dealings with government. In 2005, 47 per cent of businesses with between 10 and 49 employees accessed e-government compared with 75 per cent of businesses with 1,000 or more employees (Figure 7.13). This could be partly because the larger the company, the more likely they are to use ICT. However, the differences between businesses carrying out different economic activities suggest that other factors may influence business electronic interactions with public administrations.

The most common reason why businesses contacted public administrations electronically is to obtain information. Nearly one-half (49 per cent) of businesses with ten or more employees did so in 2005, compared with 29 per cent in 2002. The proportion that obtained forms electronically from public administrations more than doubled between 2002 and 2005, from 22 per cent to 46 per cent. More than one-third (36 per cent) used the Internet to return completed forms in 2005, compared with just less than 10 per cent in 2002.

Businesses with ten or more employees in the banking, financial and insurance sector were most likely to have electronic interactions with public administrations, 67 per cent in 2005 (Figure 7.14). Those in wholesale, retail, catering and travel were least likely, at 42 per cent.

### Figure **7.14**

**Business interactions[1] with public administrations: by broad industrial sector[2]**

**United Kingdom**

Percentages

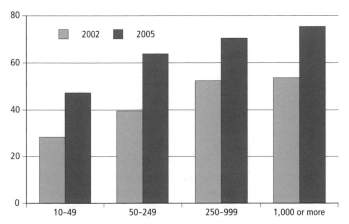

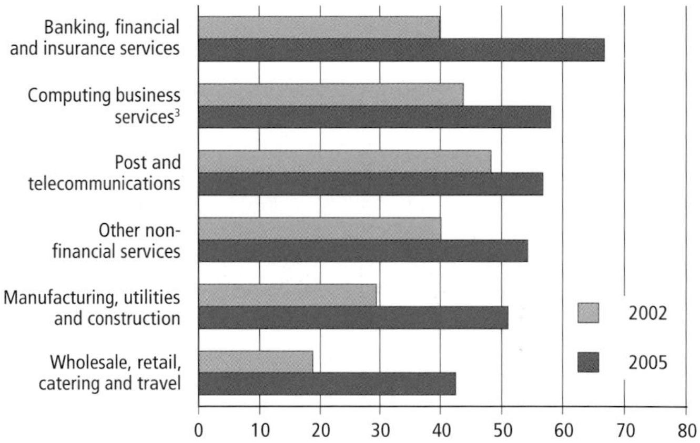

1  Including obtaining information, forms, returning forms and full case handling.
2  Businesses with ten or more employees.
3  Includes renting and real estate.

*Source: e-Commerce Survey, Office for National Statistics*

### www.businesslink.gov.uk

Businesslink.gov.uk is managed by the Department for Trade and Industry to serve a growing demand in the small business community for a single point of access with government, where information could be obtained and business returns made. Businesslink.gov.uk works with each government department to make their electronic regulatory information and guidance easy to understand, intuitive to find and easy to use. For instance, an employer browsing guidance about taking on a new employee will be directed to the *Check your legal responsibilities when taking on an employee* decision tree. Developed with five different departments, this tool helps the business to isolate and understand the issues and obligations that are specific to them. The same business may then be prompted to use a further interactive tool, *Create a written statement of employment*, where they can download and print a tailored written statement giving the legal obligations for both parties. This journey has been taken by 44,000 users since the two tools were launched in late 2004.

Businesslink.gov.uk is developing the final component of full-case handling (being able to complete the whole transaction

### Figure **7.13**

**Business interactions[1] with public administrations: by number of employees**

**United Kingdom**

Percentages

1  Including obtaining information, forms, returning forms and full case handling.

*Source: e-Commerce Survey, Office for National Statistics*

electronically) that will provide easy access to the many different interactions a business undertakes with government departments. These include registering as self-employed, registering for Value Added Tax and notifying the Information Commissioner – all activities that are currently done through posted forms, telephone helplines or discrete services at each departmental website.

## Notes and references

1   Self-service channels are channels where the customers serve themselves using menu options on a telephone system or on a web-based service, for example, rather than going through a customer service representative.

2   The Number 10 website www.pm.gov.uk/output/Page2851.asp

3   European Commission (2004), *Web Based Survey of Electronic Public Services*, p26. (http://europa.eu.int/information_society/soccul/egov/egov_benchmarking_2005.pdf)

4   The UK Government launched its new strategy in November 2005. See CIO Council (2005), *Transformational Government – enabled by technology*. www.cio.gov.uk

5   Data for e-government questions were collected in the Omnibus Survey in October 2004 and February, May and July 2005, unless otherwise specified. In other chapters in this report the 2004/05 Omnibus Survey covers May, July and October 2004 and February 2005.

6   Office for National Statistics (2005), *Time Series for reasons why people do not use the Internet*. www.statistics.gov.uk/StatBase/ssdataset.asp?vlnk=6939&Pos=&ColRank=1&Rank=432

7   The North East seems to be an outlier, with a much higher e-government user base than its Internet population would suggest. The correlation between the percentage of Internet users on a regional basis and the percentage of these regional Internet populations that visit government websites is high ($r^2 = 0.84$) if the North East is excluded, and statistically significant at the 5 per cent level. One possible explanation is that the North East, with its lower internet population, has a higher concentration of early internet adopters, who are potentially also early adopters of e-government.

8   NHS Direct Online was set out in the *NHS Plan* (July 2000) www.dh.gov.uk/publicationsAndStatistics/publications

9   The size of the business is described in terms of number of employees. This includes all in employment in the business, including the owner.

# e-Security

**Debbie Wilson**
Home Office
**Ivan Bishop**
Department of Trade and Industry

Chapter 8

## Introduction

Advances in digital technology and the increase in the use of information and communication technology (ICT) both at home and at work has meant that more computers and users are at risk of a security breach. Examples of this include viruses, hacking and financial fraud, and other problems such as offensive material sent through the Internet, email harassment, equipment theft and systems being used for criminal or illegitimate purposes such as online copyright theft. The rise in electronic crime has caused individuals, businesses and organisations in the public sector to invest in increased security and protection for their computers. It has also led to the Government introducing new legislation.

### Computer viruses and hacking

A computer virus is a computer program that is able to replicate its code in whole or in part by infecting or modifying other programs and adding to or overwriting their codes with a different code that can also infect other programs. These malicious codes, which include variants known as trojans, worms and spyware, aim to damage or compromise the ICT systems of victims, and are constantly being evolved.

Computer hacking is the unauthorised access by outsiders to a personal computer or business computer, potentially leading to theft, fraud, sabotage or disclosure of confidential information.

## Household and individual e-security

### Viruses and hacking

The 2003/04 British Crime Survey (BCS)[1] identified the effect that computer viruses had on household computers in England and Wales. More than one-quarter (27 per cent) of adults aged 16 and over who accessed the Internet at home said that their home computer had been affected by a computer virus in the previous 12 months and 9 per cent said their computer had been damaged by the virus. This compared with 18 per cent affected by a computer virus in 2002/03, the first year that the BCS included questions on technology crime. Of those affected in 2003/04, 37 per cent had reported it: 9 per cent to an Internet service provider; 6 per cent to a website or systems administrator; and 1 per cent to the police.

According to the 2003 Offending, Crime and Justice Survey (OCJS),[2] which also covers England and Wales, the figures for offenders were much lower. Less than 1 per cent of respondents aged between 10 and 65 who had used the Internet had knowingly sent a computer virus in the last 12 months. However, with this type of offence a small number of offenders can have an impact on a large number of victims.

As with virus infections there is little research on how many home computers have been affected by computer hacking. Results from the BCS indicated that 2 per cent of adults who used the Internet at home thought that someone had accessed or hacked into files on their home computer in the last 12 months. Of these 18 per cent had reported the incident to an Internet service provider and 5 per cent to a systems administrator. No one had reported it to the police.

The OCJS figures on self-reported offending show that less than 1 per cent of Internet users had used the Internet to hack into other computers. Around one-half of these (0.5 per cent of Internet users) admitted to hacking and sending a computer virus, 0.4 per cent admitted to just computer hacking, and 0.4 per cent to only sending computer viruses.

### Offensive material through the Internet

One in eight (12 per cent) BCS respondents aged 16 and over who accessed the Internet on their home computer had received a message by email that they considered offensive or that constituted harassment in the 12 months before interview. This was equivalent to 5 per cent of the adult population. Of those victimised in this manner 31 per cent reported it to someone. Less than 1 per cent of OCJS respondents aged between 10 and 65 admitted causing harassment through emails. However, as with sending viruses, one offender can have multiple victims.

More than one-third of adults (34 per cent) who used the Internet at home were worried about their household accessing or receiving offensive, pornographic or threatening material over the Internet on their home computer, with 11 per cent very worried and 23 per cent fairly worried. Women were slightly more worried than men about receiving such material (36 per cent compared with 33 per cent). Adults with children in the household were more likely to be worried, 45 per cent compared with 27 per cent of adults without children.

Around one-quarter of adults who used the Internet at home had unintentionally accessed or received offensive or upsetting unsolicited material in the previous 12 months. The proportion may be higher than this as the respondent answering the question may not know if this had happened to another member of the household. Of those respondents who had received offensive or upsetting unsolicited material 18 per cent had reported it to someone, with 2 per cent reporting it to the police.

In 2003/04, 39 per cent of people who used the Internet at home had taken measures to stop household members accessing or receiving offensive, pornographic or threatening material. Of those households that had received or accessed unsolicited or upsetting material on their home computer in the past 12 months, 61 per cent had taken measures to prevent this happening. This compared with 26 per cent of those who used the Internet at home and had not received or accessed such material. The Survey did not establish whether the precautions were taken before or after receipt of or access to the material.[3]

The most common security measures taken by households on their home computers were blocks/filters on email, these are used by 23 per cent of all households in England and Wales where the respondent used the Internet at home (Figure 8.1). This was up from 16 per cent in 2002/03. Other common measures, taken by 19 per cent of households in 2003/04, were placing controls, restrictions or blocks in the browser/service provider/search engine.

## Figure **8.1**

### Measures taken in households[1] to stop access to or receipt of offensive Internet material, 2003/04

**England and Wales**

Percentages

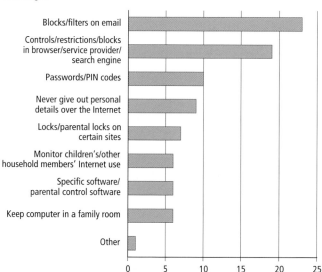

1  Based on households where the respondents used the Internet at home.

*Source: British Crime Survey, Home Office*

## Copyright theft

Copyright theft is not a new crime. However, with technological advances and an increase in Internet access at home, online copyright theft has become a new form of this type of criminal activity. It involves music, software (the programs that tell the computer how to process the data, see text box entitled Computer hardware and software for definitions on page 34) or movies being illegally placed on the Internet, which enables others to share and illegally download. The 2003 OCJS found that 15 per cent of respondents who

had used the Internet during the last 12 months had illegally downloaded software or music that they knew to be pirated or otherwise unauthorised.

Of all the technology crimes, copyright theft had the highest prevalence. Males were more likely to commit copyright theft than females, 20 per cent compared with 9 per cent. Younger respondents (aged 25 and under) were more likely to do this than older respondents. Those in full-time education were more likely than those in any other work status category.

## Businesses and e-security

The 2006 Information Security Breaches Survey (ISBS)[4] found that more than one-half of businesses (52 per cent) in the UK had a malicious or premeditated e-security incident during 2005 (Figure 8.2). This had fallen from 68 per cent of businesses in 2003, but was higher than in 2001 (44 per cent). Large businesses (those with 250 or more employees) were especially likely to fall victim, with 84 per cent suffering a malicious or premeditated incident in 2005.

## Figure **8.2**

### Businesses that had a malicious security incident[1]

**United Kingdom**

Percentages

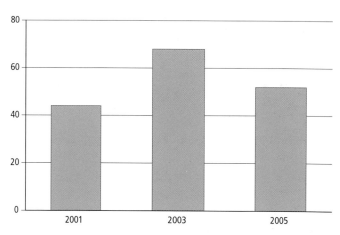

1  During the year.

*Source: Information Security Breaches Survey, Department of Trade and Industry*

According to the ISBS, slightly less than one-half of all businesses that had an e-security incident considered their worst one to be serious in the sense that it caused significant disruption or cost to business. Among large businesses slightly more than one-half had a serious breach.

UK businesses had to deal with a median[5] of five malicious e-security incidents in 2005, up from four in 2003, with large businesses dealing with a median of 16. This was down from 29 in 2003. It cost UK businesses an estimated average cost of between £8,000 and £17,000 to deal with the worst e-security incident they had in 2005. Large companies faced higher costs from their worst incident, between £65,000 and £130,000. The ISBS estimated that for UK businesses overall, the cost of security breaches in 2005 was around 50 per cent higher than in 2003, though the cost to large companies had fallen to about half the level they suffered in 2003, suggesting that an increasing proportion of the overall burden was falling on small and medium-sized enterprises.

## Categories of impact

The ISBS looked at four categories of impact in estimating the cost of e-security breaches: business disruption; incident response costs; direct financial losses; and damage to reputation (see text box entitled Categories of impact). While for certain specific incidents businesses suffered considerable incident response costs and direct financial losses, on average business disruption accounted for around three-quarters of the total cost of the worst e-security breach that businesses faced.

### Categories of impact

**Business disruption** Interruption to normal service, such as loss of access to systems or loss of connections with customers

**Incident response costs** The cost of investigating and repairing the damage done by a security breach

**Direct financial losses** The cost of fines or compensation payments resulting from e-security breaches, for example, of confidentiality and losses from fraud, and physical theft of ICT

**Damage to reputation** The loss of customer or partner trust in the business following failure to provide a service, protect confidential information or resist Internet fraud

The Hi-Tech Crime Survey (HTCS), commissioned by the National Hi-Tech Crime Unit,[6] estimated that the minimum total cost of impact of computer crime on UK-located companies with over 1,000 employees was £2.4 billion in 2004, while for businesses with between 100 and 1,000 employees the cost was £177 million. Among firms with over 1,000 employees more than one-half of the estimated costs of computer enabled crime came from two main types of criminal activity: planting viruses, worms or trojans (28 per cent) and financial fraud (25 per cent), together costing an estimated £1.2 billion (Table 8.3). These two sources also accounted for 78 per cent of the estimated costs of computer crime to firms with between 100 and 1,000 employees, 40 per cent and 38 per cent respectively, costing an estimated £139 million.

Table **8.3**

### Estimated total cost of computer-enabled crime: by type of crime, 2004

United Kingdom

£ million

| | Firms with 100 to 1,000 employees | Firms with over 1,000 employees |
|---|---|---|
| Viruses, worms or trojans | 70.8 | 676.7 |
| Financial fraud | 68.2 | 622.3 |
| Denial of service | 2.9 | 555.2 |
| Equipment theft | 28.8 | 383.7 |
| Telecoms fraud | 0.1 | 77.7 |
| Systems used for criminal/ illegitimate purposes | 0.2 | 46.1 |
| Unauthorised access to business system | 2.2 | 43.7 |
| Theft of information/data | 3.3 | 33.3 |
| Sabotage of data or networks | 0.7 | 5.7 |
| Website defacement | 0.1 | - |

*Source: Hi-Tech Crime Survey, Serious Organised Crime Agency*

Two-thirds of respondents to the HTCS identified that their greatest concern when assessing the impact of computer enabled crime was whether the company was able to continue to function and carry on business with its customers. Around one in six were most concerned about the impact on the public image or reputation of the company, while nearly one in eight were primarily worried by the potential impact on company finances.

## Types of e-security breach

The ISBS investigated the occurrence of four types of malicious e-security breach: virus infection and disruptive software; staff misuse of information systems; unauthorised access by outsiders; and theft and fraud involving computers (see text box entitled Types of malicious e-security breaches).

For each type of malicious e-security incident the proportion of UK businesses targeted in 2005 either fell or remained the same compared with 2003. This is in contrast to the significant increases reported for each type of incident between 2001 and 2003. The proportion of businesses infected by viruses or other disruptive software fell from one-half (50 per cent) in 2003 to around one-third (35 per cent) in 2005, lower than the level in 2001 (41 per cent), while the proportion facing theft and fraud involving computers went down from 11 per cent in 2003 to 8 per cent in 2005 (Figure 8.4). There was little change in the proportion of UK businesses suffering staff misuse of information

## Types of malicious e-security breach

**Virus infection and disruptive software** These are often attached to spam emails (unsolicited, unwanted, irrelevant or inappropriate messages) and the threats are constantly being evolved. Denial of service attacks, where businesses are bombarded by emails, are also increasing. See also text box entitled Computer viruses and hacking at the beginning of the chapter

**Staff misuse of information systems** Excessive personal email use, access to inappropriate websites, excessive web surfing, sending inappropriate email or email containing confidential information, and using another person's ID to access systems

**Unauthorised access by outsiders** Attempts by hackers (scanning and probing) to break into business systems, Internet or telecommunications, potentially leading to unauthorised disclosure or theft of confidential information

**Theft and fraud involving computers** Physical theft of computer equipment and fraud using computer systems, including authentication theft

systems, from 22 per cent to 21 per cent, and no change from 2003 for businesses facing attacks by unauthorised outsiders (around 17 per cent).

A higher proportion of large businesses with 250 or more employees had their systems infected by a virus, 43 per cent compared with 35 per cent of UK businesses overall in 2005.

## Figure **8.4**

### Businesses suffering malicious e-security incident: by type of incident

**United Kingdom**

Percentages

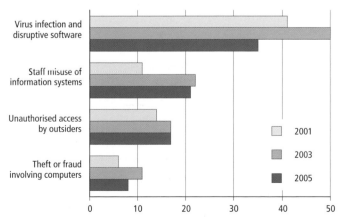

*Source: Information Security Breaches Survey, Department of Trade and Industry*

Although one in five businesses were affected by staff misuse of their IT systems in 2005, nearly two-thirds of large companies were affected by this type of incident. Businesses that were affected by staff misuse had a median of seven such incidents during 2003, although 4 per cent of affected businesses reported hundreds of incidents of misuse of web access a day. Nearly one-half (44 per cent) of large businesses compared with 8 per cent of all UK businesses had to deal with theft or fraud involving computers. Physical theft of computer equipment tended to be an isolated incident, with around 8 per cent of businesses falling victim in 2005. Of these, 86 per cent suffered from one incident. Fraud or theft over computer networks was rarer, affecting 1 per cent of businesses. However, for the small proportion affected it proved serious, with all of those suffering a computer fraud identifying it as the worst security breach of the year.

The ISBS estimated that just over one-third of UK businesses were infected by a virus or other disruptive software in 2005, and these businesses suffered a median of three infections during the year. Of the businesses affected, large businesses were more likely to suffer multiple virus attacks. The HTCS found that businesses with over 100 employees received a median seven virus, trojan or worm attacks a day in 2004, with more than one-third causing no infection of company systems. However, organisations with over 10,000 employees suffered damage to their business systems from such attacks every three days, on average. Because of the large number of incidents, virus, trojan or worm attacks exacted the highest overall cost to recover from for businesses with between 100 and 1,000 employees and those with over 1,000 employees, see Table 8.3.

Nearly one-third (32 per cent) of the businesses infected by a virus attack in 2005 were infected once, while 56 per cent were infected a few times during the year and 4 per cent suffered from infections at least once a day (Figure 8.5). Relatively few businesses, 5 per cent, were affected by a denial of service attack in 2005, down from around 7 per cent in 2003. However, nearly one-half (47 per cent) of those businesses affected were targeted more than once, with 4 per cent attacked at least once a day. The cost of these incidents to businesses with over 1,000 employees was high, reaching an estimated £550 million in 2005, demonstrating the seriousness of individual attacks.

The HTCS found that both financial fraud and equipment theft were also among the most costly types of computer related crime to affect businesses. Businesses with over 1,000 employees were hit by estimated costs of more than £600 million from financial fraud and slightly less than £400 million from equipment theft in 2004, while those with between 100 and 1,000 employees faced estimated costs of just less than

## Figure **8.5**

### Frequency of virus attacks on businesses, 2005

**United Kingdom**

Percentages

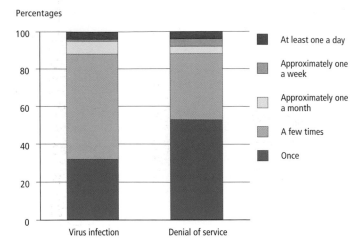

*Source: Information Security Breaches Survey, Department of Trade and Industry*

£70 million from financial fraud and around £30 million from equipment theft. Again the relatively high cost of individual incidents is emphasised, given the small number of incidents of these types of computer crime.

Around one in six UK businesses, and nearly one-third of large businesses, faced an attempt to gain unauthorised access to their IT systems (including denial of service attacks) in 2005, according to the ISBS, with 2 per cent of businesses suffering from unauthorised penetration of their network. Of these four in five suffered a single breach. Two per cent were affected by attacks on their communications traffic. Of these nearly two-thirds suffered one attack while one in ten reported hundreds of attacks a day. Three per cent of businesses were affected by impersonation of their company on the Internet, for example, false websites, and more than one-half of these were affected by more than one attack of this type.

Both the ISBS and HTCS reported that the majority of computer-related crime originated from external sources, especially so in the case of denial of service or virus attacks. However the amount of hi-tech crime committed by people from inside the business affected was statistically significant. Around two-thirds of incidents in small businesses were generated externally in 2003, while for large businesses one-half were generated externally and one-half from the inside, according to the ISBS 2004 report.

Around three in ten UK businesses were affected by accidental security incidents such as systems failure or data corruption in 2005, slightly more than in 2003. The median number of such incidents suffered by those affected remained unchanged at two a year, while for large businesses it fell from four to three.

Hardware (the physical parts of the computer, see text box entitled Computer hardware and software on page 34 for definition) failure accounted for more than half of these types of incidents. Although these incidents were usually isolated, they were often statistically significant; around one in five businesses suffering an e-security incident in 2005 reported hardware failure as the cause of their worst incident.

## Legislation relating to e-security

In the UK and internationally, governments have passed legislation and businesses have developed e-security management standards aimed at improving the level of trust in computer systems and trading online, and improving the level of security management carried out by businesses.[7]

There is a range of legislation in the UK that covers the electronic monitoring of staff. The earliest was the *Computer Misuse Act 1990* and others include the *Data Protection Act 1998* and the *Freedom of Information Act 2000*.

The *Computer Misuse Act 1990* legislates against the threat of unauthorised access to computer material, making it an offence to try and secure access to any program or data held on a computer when knowingly unauthorised to do so. The Act also covered the introduction of harmful worms and viruses to a system. The punishment for such an offence is a custodial sentence, but not exceeding five years.

The *Data Protection Act 1998* covers the processing of personal information and places a legal obligation on data controllers. Those processing personal information are required to take appropriate technical and organisational measures against unauthorised or unlawful processing of the information, and against accidental loss or damage to the information.

The *Freedom of Information Act 2000* is designed to give people easy access to information from public sector organisations, such as central and local government, the emergency services, and health and education departments. This does not affect private sector organisations.

Some legislation has been aimed at improving the ability of organisations to trade securely across the EU. The Electronic Signatures EC Directive 1999, largely enacted into UK law by the *Electronic Communications Act 2000*, introduced a uniform standard for legal recognition of electronic signatures regardless of their origin in the EU, and facilitated the legal recognition of electronic writing.

The Privacy and Electronic Communications (EC Directive) Regulations 2003 cover a number of issues relating to privacy in respect of e-communication, including topics such as telemarketing and the use of 'cookies' (which are files placed on a user's system when visiting a website that contain information about the user and an identification in the event of a revisit to the site). The Regulation requires that for cookies to be allowed, the user must be told about the purpose and storage of, and have access to, the information contained. The user should also have the opportunity to decline the storage of that information.

## Best practice guidelines relating to e-security

As well as legislation, there has been a concerted effort to provide best practice guidance on e-security management to businesses. The British Standard for Information Security Management (BS 7799) has been available since 1995.[8] Part 1 of the Standard contains guidance and explanatory information, and became an International Standard (ISO/IEC 17799) in December 2000. Part 2 provides a model for an information security management system, and became an International Standard (ISO/IEC 27001) in October 2005.

BS 7799 Part 1 provides guidance in ten sections, each covering a particular aspect of an information security management system, such as having a security policy, how security management will be organised within the business, access controls, legal compliance and continuity management.

### Business management of e-security

Four in ten (40 per cent) of UK businesses had a formal information security policy in place by the end of 2005, according to the ISBS, up from one-third (34 per cent) in 2003 (Figure 8.6). Large businesses were more likely to have one, with nearly three-quarters (73 per cent) of companies employing 250 or more having a policy in 2005.

In 2005 nearly two-thirds (65 per cent) of UK businesses had documented procedures to ensure compliance with the *Data Protection Act 1998*, up from 47 per cent in 2003. A further 9 per cent of businesses were planning to introduce them.

One in ten of those responsible for e-security in UK businesses were aware of the contents of BS 7799 in 2005, though among large companies this rose to nearly four in ten. The ISBS suggests that the pricing and distribution of BS 7799 could be a barrier as there was a demand among those unaware of BS 7799 for wider promotion of information security management standards.

Two-thirds of businesses (67 per cent) that were aware of BS7799 were partly or completely compliant with the Standard in 2005, up from 59 per cent in 2030. Among those implementing BS 7799, around 90 per cent believed that they

Figure **8.6**

**Businesses with a formal information security policy**

United Kingdom

Percentages

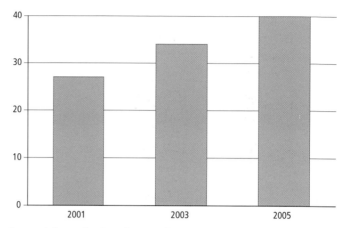

Source: Information Security Breaches Survey, Department of Trade and Industry

had obtained benefits from it. For 30 per cent the biggest benefit was greater security awareness, while for 17 per cent marketing opportunities were the biggest gain.

In 2005, 12 per cent of UK businesses had staff with a specialist information security qualification, a similar proportion to 2003 (11 per cent). Large businesses were more likely to have such qualified staff, with 29 per cent in 2005, up from 25 per cent in 2003. The person responsible for information security had a formal relevant qualification in 3 per cent of businesses and in 6 per cent of large businesses in 2005 (Figure 8.7). Most businesses (88 per cent) had no one with formal information security qualifications. However, in recent years specific information security qualifications, including an MSc and professional qualifications such as Certified Information Systems Security Professionals (CISSP), Certified Information Security Managers (CISM) and CISCO Certification, have been developed, so there is a likelihood of growth in staff with information security qualifications once these courses become established.

The majority of UK businesses (96 per cent) obtained external security advice in 2005. The most popular source, personal contacts within the business or security community, was used by 42 per cent. Other sources commonly consulted were external auditors and IT service providers or consultancies. Many businesses used external advice to fill gaps in security expertise (being too small to afford in-house security specialists).

## Figure **8.7**

### Businesses with an information security team: by whether any team members have formal IT or information security qualifications, 2005

**United Kingdom**

Percentages

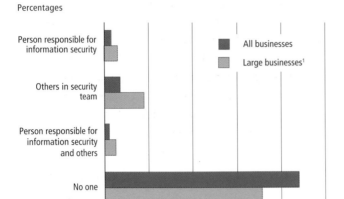

1   250 or more employees.

*Source: Information Security Breaches Survey, Department of Trade and Industry*

The ISBS found that over four in ten businesses increased their security spend in 2005, while one in fifty reduced expenditure. On average firms spent between 4 and 5 per cent of their IT budget on e-security, up from 3 per cent in 2003. Large businesses spent an average of 6 to 8 per cent.

Around one in ten UK businesses spent over 10 per cent of their IT budget on information security, while one-quarter spent 1 per cent or less and 14 per cent spent nothing on information security. Businesses that were most likely to spend a higher proportion of their IT budget on e-security were those where the senior management gave a high priority to e-security, those that had carried out a risk assessment and those that had experienced security incidents.

Less than three in ten UK businesses measured the return on investment on e-security expenditure in 2005, although more than one-half had prepared formal business cases or quantified the benefits of e-security expenditure (often doing both). The main reasons why businesses invested in e-security were to protect the data they held, and their reputation. Five motivations were identified by around nine in ten businesses as important or very important reasons for e-security: protecting customer information; maintaining data integrity; protecting the organisation's reputation; maintaining continuity in disaster situation; and complying with laws and regulations.

Almost every business in the UK (98 per cent) that connected to the Internet in 2005 had anti-virus software, and this rose to 100 per cent for large businesses. Four in five also updated

their anti-virus at least daily, although most businesses had sophisticated anti-virus software, making them less dependent on immediate updates to guard against threats.

Businesses have various policies to counter inappropriate use of the Internet or email by employees and some use more than one method. In 2005 nearly two-thirds (63 per cent) of UK businesses had an acceptable usage policy, 42 per cent restricted use of the Internet to certain staff, the same proportion logged and monitored sites that employees accessed and 38 per cent blocked access to inappropriate sites (Figure 8.8). Large businesses were most likely of all businesses to have policies on Internet use: nine in ten had an acceptable usage policy, around one-half restricted staff access, four in five monitored staff usage, and three-quarters blocked inappropriate sites.

To control access to their computer systems, more than nine in ten UK businesses employed single factor user-ID passwords in 2005. Less than one in twenty used strong authentication techniques such as a smart card or biometrics,[9] leaving their systems potentially vulnerable. These strong authentication techniques reduced the number of unauthorised access incidents. The ISBS found that using software second factor authentication, for example software tokens or digital certificates, with IDs and passwords did not lead to a reduction in unauthorised access breaches.

In 2005, nine in ten businesses with a website that was managed in-house used a firewall to defend it, with four in five adding intrusion detection software to their defences.

## Figure **8.8**

### How businesses control staff internet usage, 2005

**United Kingdom**

Percentages

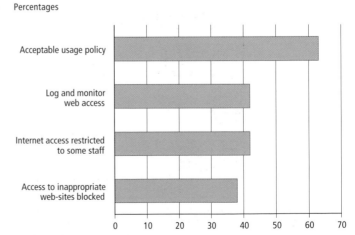

*Source: Information Security Breaches Survey, Department of Trade and Industry*

However, nearly nine in ten businesses with a website had it hosted externally (61 per cent of large businesses) and placed the onus for security on the service provider. Less than three in ten businesses (and less than one-half of large businesses) with websites hosted externally knew what security controls their service provider used.

By 2005 more than one-third of UK businesses enabled staff to have remote access to their systems. Of these 60 per cent used additional passwords to give staff remote access, up 42 per cent in 2003 (Figure 8.9). Four in ten businesses (40 per cent) that allowed staff remote access encrypted their transmissions using virtual private network technology, up from 24 per cent in 2003. Nearly one-fifth (18 per cent) had no additional security controls for staff accessing their systems remotely in 2005 compared with more than one-quarter (27 per cent) in 2003.

One-quarter of businesses had implemented wireless networks by the end of 2005. Of these nearly six in ten used encrypted signals for protection. Other techniques, such as secure placement of access points and restriction of connections to known computers, were also used. One in five businesses with a wireless network had not put in place any e-security controls.

Businesses try to limit the damage from accidental security incidents. Nearly six in ten UK businesses had a disaster recovery plan in place in 2005, while nearly all businesses backed up critical data, 78 per cent at least daily. More than three-quarters of businesses stored their backup off-site.

## Figure **8.9**

### Businesses providing remote access: by additional security controls

**United Kingdom**

Percentages

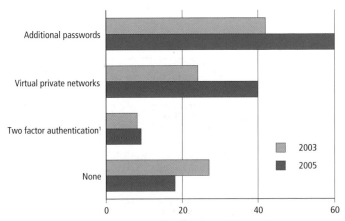

1  Two factor authentication (TFA) is any authentication process that requires two independent ways to establish identity and privileges.

*Source: Information Security Breaches Survey, Department of Trade and Industry*

## Notes and references

1  The British Crime Survey (BCS) is a large, nationally representative, household victimisation survey that has been conducted since 1982. Its main purpose is to measure the extent and nature of criminal victimisation against adults aged 16 or over living in private households in England and Wales. The 2002/03 BCS included questions on technology crime and victimisation for the first time. The 2003/04 BCS reports on 42,285 interviews conducted between April 2003 and March 2004 and refers to incidents experienced by respondents in the 12 months before interview. Interviews were conducted face to face by trained interviewers. The response rate was 74 per cent. Further information on the BCS can be found at: www.homeoffice.gov.uk/rds/bcs1.html

2  The 2003 Offending, Crime and Justice Survey (OCJS) had a random probability sample design. The main survey comprised 10,079 people aged 10 to 65 living in private houses in England and Wales. The response rate for the main sample was 74 per cent. Fieldwork took place between January and July 2003. The first part of the interview was interviewer-administered; the second part, including the more sensitive questions, was self-administered. The 2003 OCJS included questions on technology crime for the first time. The 2004 OCJS only covered young people aged between 10 and 25 so the 2003 survey has been used in this report. Further information on the Offending, Crime and Justice Survey can be found at: www.homeoffice.gov.uk/rds/offending_survey.html

3  Figures from Wilson D (ed) (2005) *Fraud and technology crimes: findings from the 2002/03 British Crime Survey and 2003 Offending, Crime and Justice Survey.* Home Office Online Report 34/05. Home Office: London. www.homeoffice.gov.uk/rds/pdfs05/rdsolr3405.pdf and Wilson D, Patterson A, Powell G and Hembury R (2006) *Fraud and technology crimes. Findings from the 2003/04 British Crime Survey, the 2004 Offending, Crime and Justice Survey and administrative sources.* Home Office Online Report 09/06. Home Office: London. www.homeoffice.gov.uk/rds/pdfs06/rdsolr0906.pdf

4  PriceWaterhouseCoopers, Department of Trade and Industry, *Information Security Breaches Survey 2006.* Interviewing for the ISBS 2006 was conducted between October 2005 and January 2006. While results relating to activities affecting the business 'in the past year' might not exactly correspond to the 2005 calendar year, they are likely to be a fairly close approximation, and therefore to improve readability the text refers to 2005. Further information on the Information Security Breaches Survey can be found at: www.dti.gov.uk/files/file28343.pdf

5   The median is the middle point, with exactly the same number
    of data values above and below. The median is often used to
    show the middle point where data are skewed or contain outliers
    (results that greatly differ from others in the same sample).

6.  NOP World, National *Hi-Tech Crime Unit, Hi-Tech Crime: The
    Impact on UK Business 2005*. The National Hi-Tech Crime Unit was
    set up in 2001 as part of the National Crime Squad. It became
    part of the Serious Organised Crime Agency in 2006.

7   Department of Trade and Industry Information Security Fact Sheet
    2005, *Legislation*.
    www.dti.gov.uk/files/file9956.pdf?pubpdfdload=05%2F628

8   Department of Trade and Industry Information Security Fact Sheet
    2005, *Understanding BS* 7799.
    www.dti.gov.uk/files/file9940.pdf?pubpdfdload=05%2F616

9   Biometrics is the automated means of recognising a living
    person through the measurement of distinguishing physiological
    or behavioural traits. It can be used for identification and
    authentication purposes.